Family Survival Guide for Our Changing Climate

52 Empowering Actions You and Your Family Can Take Now!

Sandi Sturm

Copyright © 2020 by Sandi Sturm

www.EarthFocusGroup.com

All rights reserved.

First Printing, 2020

The information in this eBook was correct at the time of publication, but the Author does not assume any liability for loss or damage caused by errors or omissions.

No part of this book may be reproduced or used in any manner without the prior written permission of the copyright owner, except for the use of brief quotations in a book review.

ISBN: 9798570528970
Imprint: Independently published

Dedication

This book is dedicated to my husband, Wayne, who has supported all my crazy ideas for the past 35 years and counting. To my daughter, Shana, and granddaughters, Tyler, and Breanna, for their ability to motivate me through love. To all species that live on earth because life would not be worth living without them.

Do you want to better understand the effects of climate change? You are invited to watch a special Video Presentation titled:

"Preparing Your Family For A Changing Climate"

During this FREE Video Presentation, which is divided into three short modules, you discover the answers every parent needs to know, including:

- → A deeper understanding of climate science 101
- → Effects of Climate Change on natural systems
- → Effects of Climate Change on your family
- → Solutions from around the world that are making a difference
- → What you can do next

So, if you're serious about wanting to better understand the effects of climate change and be a superhero to your children, register now for this free video series that shows you why we need to reduce our emissions 50% by 2030.

Get Access Now!

https://Book.EarthPrintsForFamilies.com

Table of Contents

Introduction VII
Background 1
52 Empowering Actions 14
1: Does Your Bank Invest In Fossil Fuel Companies? 15
2: Decorating The Landfill 18
3: Compost Reduces Methane 22
4: Carbon Conscious Night Out 25
5: Grow It, Don't Mow It 29
6: From The Farm To Your Table 33
7: Food On The Go 37
8: Experiences Instead Of Stuff 40
9: Electric Vehicles Today 42
10: Saga Of The Glass Bottle 46
11: Put Your Mailbox On A Diet 50
12: Paper Free Vendors 53
13: Let There Be Light 56
14: Is That New? 60
15: The Sun May Save You 63
16: The Meat Connection 66

Family Survival Guide

17: The Community Tool Shed 70
18: Sustainable And Conscious Gatherings 73
19: Say No To Plastic Bags 76
20: Your Laundry Is Out To Get You 78
21: What Are Carbon Offsets? 83
22: Waste Not So Others Want Not 86
23: There's Oil In My Disposable Water Bottle? 90
24: Write For Your Rights 93
25: Gifts Of Time 95
26: Bring Back The Picnic Basket 98
27: Driving For Clean Air 100
28: Xeriscaping 103
29: Join A Group 106
30: Give It The Green Business 108
31: Comment Boxes 111
32: Green Hotels 113
33: Eco Swap 116
34: Fast Fashion 118
35: Battle Of The Plants 121
36: Open The Door, Not Just The Window 125
37: The Gift Of Sight 128
38: Are Your Electronics Hazardous? 130
39: Close, Unplug And Turn Off 135

Family Survival Guide

40: Colorful Hazards 140
41: Experiences For Parents And Grandparents 142
42: Home Sweet Home 144
43: Put A Blanket On It 148
44: Love Of Your Furniture 152
45: Buying For Baby 155
46: Driving Carbon Free 159
47: What Is The Deal With Palm Oil? 163
48: Cooling It Down Is Heating Us Up 167
49: It May Sound Good At First 171
50: Be A Trainer 174
51: Just Park Already 177
52 179
Notes 181
About The Author 189

Introduction

Why do I believe in Climate Change and why did I write this book?

Before I applied to take the Climate Reality Leadership Training with Former Vice President and Nobel Peace Prize winner Al Gore, I was asked that very question.

In searching for the answer to this question I revisited many paths that lead me to where I am today. My love of nature must have come from the trips to my grandparents cabin every other week from the time I was seven or eight.

They retired into the woods within the Ozarks of Missouri near the Huzzah River. It was a short two-hour drive from our home in Illinois, crossing the Mississippi River and wrangling through the highways of St. Louis, until finally you hit a sea of deciduous forests and rolling hills. This is where I learned to swim, shoot a 22 rifle, and pick berries.

My cousins and I would spend most of the day outdoors exploring the abundant woods and berry patches. Grandma had a garden that grew quite well in the rocky soil, and grandpa would hunt for wild turkey, squirrel, and rabbit.

When the family gathered there was always a fish fry followed by a serious poker game. We kids were not allowed at the table, but it was not difficult to entertain ourselves.

My contribution was playing with the tadpoles they used for fish bait and making disgusting remarks about the occasional pig that was turning over an open fire.

Food was cooked on an old iron wood-burning stove that provided a smell of woodsmoke as the morning biscuits baked and coffee perked. Those aromas still calm me today.

That is what wild meant to me.

I took this love of wilderness along with me into my adult years. Now I explore National Parks and am more at ease on the road in a motor home than somewhere growing roots.

After a bit more thought about that question – "Why do I believe in Climate Change"- I realized that I have enjoyed many freedoms during my life and the one I have enjoyed most is location freedom. Wayne, my husband, and I have been fortunate to have lived in some beautiful places and spend a lot of our time on the road in our motor home. In fact, we figure we pulled our previous travel trailer about a quarter-million miles. *

All those miles looking through the windshield and stopping to examine hundreds of points of interest, has given me a unique personal perspective – an experiential visualization to reference beyond the news.

As I write this, we are parked in Mesa, Arizona. This region is heavily impacted by drought and changes in weather patterns. Summers are hotter and longer and winters are cooler than in people's recent memories. I keep hearing

Family Survival Guide

people say, "This is the coldest winter we have ever experienced in the past 20 years we have been coming here."

Yet, every empty lot has construction vehicles building mega complexes for the winter visitors. And most of those have 9 – 27-hole golf courses. Saudi Arabians are also buying up land at very premium prices to grow alfalfa for their cattle, so they do not have to use their own water.

Just upstream Hoover Dam and Lake Mead are at half capacity. When will this sink in?

I feel the sadness and suffering of those displaced by the ever-increasing climate-related "inconveniences," because I witness many of those climate-related events. Maybe the people here in the four corners area of the U.S. are not yet inconvenienced enough to change.

We have seen many of the results that our changing climate is forcing on us.

Imagine having an hours' notice to pack up your belongings and escape a wildfire. We have witnessed more than one such event. A visual that haunts me still is seeing families pull out of their driveways in Yukon, Canada with the back of their truck loaded with possessions, knowing that what remains will be ash by morning.

The true look of fear in the eyes of the parents grabbing on to their children, not wanting them to know what the future may hold for them as they flee through smoke and flames that now overtake their neighborhood.

Family Survival Guide

This scenario is repeated day after day as the western US and other regions of the world battle more and more wildfires.

We spent the summer in Oregon about 10 miles from wildfires that burned entire communities. The air was not healthy to breath, but at least I still have a place to call home. We did not leave because we were surrounded by wildfires on all sides and there really was no place to escape.

Watching the news of Gatlinburg, Tennessee on fire a few years ago hit my heart as we worked with many of the small business owners who lost their shops and some, even their homes. This was not just a news story - it was a personal emotional experience.

When storms hit the Florida coast and flood waters rise inside living rooms, I can visualize times spent with family on that very couch that is now ankle deep in yuck and know how their lives are turned upside down for weeks to come, if they are lucky enough to have a living room left to return to. The 2020 hurricane season is breaking a lot of records, so this is a cycle that is not ending any time soon.

I have watched houses fall into melting glacier fed rivers in Alaska because of extremely high temperatures melting the glacier a few miles upstream; homes where families raised their children and hugged their grandchildren for the past 25 years or more.

I have heard personal stories of stranded polar bears in villages where I once walked. Those same villages now unable

Family Survival Guide

to get their subsistence salmon because the salmon are not returning.

As California and the west is burning, I can visualize natural places that will never be as they were: Giant redwoods, clean, clear waterfalls, and pristine skies. So many lives lost, and lives of the survivors changed forever as they become climate refugees.

In a two-month span of time in 2018, Wayne and I were evacuated in our travel trailer from two wildfires in Oregon. We were the lucky ones because we were able to bring our home with us. Residents were not so lucky, and the local economy was also greatly affected, just as our personal income was affected.

We have many such stories – too many to ignore. Yet, there are still deniers.

Maybe due to fear. Maybe because it is inconvenient. It certainly is inconvenient to the millions of people around the world already displaced due to climate-related events. It is becoming very personal. In fact, if you had 100 people in a room and ask them to raise their hand if they know of someone who has been affected by wildfires, floods, storms or other climate-related disasters, there will be many hands in the air.

This is why I believe in climate change. This is why we want to empower you with 52 ways to reduce your family's carbon footprint. We believe people need to be educated, as well as given hope. Because there is still hope. Therefore, I am writing this book for you and your family.

I believe and I acknowledge that we are all capable of making the change we need to make. And I do this work for the future of my family, friends, your family, your friends, and you.

Do not be the frog in the boiling pot – eventually the heat will become uninhabitable – Act as if your life depends on it, because it does.

Sandi Sturm
Virgin, Utah
November 2020

*I know, some of you are saying Wow, you contributed a lot of carbon in your travels! Yes, from our vehicle, but we lived in 160 square feet and did this over a 20-year period. We also can and do purchase carbon credits to offset the emissions. Now we park the motor home for 2-3 months per location and drive our electric tow vehicle.

This book has two main sections.

This first section gives you some vocabulary and background information on the topic of Climate Change.

As a special bonus, you can go to this website to watch a more in-depth video series showing the information presented here, the results of climate change, and some great success stories.

https://book.EarthPrintsForFamilies.com

To wrap up you will find 52 empowering actions you can take to personally reduce your carbon footprint. I have also added some ideas you can share with your community. Big changes do come from the actions of individuals.

Background

Our Atmosphere, Our Home

Can you imagine looking out the window to see a full view of our planet for the very first time? On December 7, 1972, astronauts on the Apollo 17 mission saw this view out of their window as they travelled towards the moon. This was the first photograph of the earth fully illuminated.

No other photograph has changed humanity the way this one did. It changed the way we thought about our home.

The image shows how thin the atmosphere is that sustains all life on earth. In fact, if you drive at highway speeds straight up, you can reach the end of the troposphere in less than 10 minutes.

But evidently, when most of us look up, we see limitless amounts of space instead of this thin shell, because we have been polluting it for many decades. In fact, we dump approximately 115 Million Tons of manmade global warming pollution [greenhouse gases] into the atmosphere every 24 hours.

As stated by James Hansen, Former Director of NASA Goddard Institute for Space Studies, "The energy trapped by man-made global warming pollution is now ... equivalent to exploding 500,000 Hiroshima atomic bombs per day, 365 days per year."

How can that be?

CO2 (Carbon Dioxide), the most present greenhouse gas, is being released into the atmosphere faster than at any time in at least the last 66 million years. The largest source is from the burning of fossil fuels. We will dig in deeper into sources and define greenhouse gases in later sections.

Why is this a problem?

For you and your family to live on this planet, we need to have earth's systems working correctly. Our atmosphere allows solar radiation (energy) to pass through in the form of light waves, with the earth absorbing most of this energy. Some of it bounces back into space as infrared waves (heat). Some of the infrared radiation (our heat) is trapped by our atmosphere which makes it "just right" for all life on earth, like baby bear exclaims in the children's story of The Three Bears. (see illustration 1)

As we dump those millions of tons of manmade pollution into our thin layer of living space, the CO2 concentration increases, along with other greenhouse gases, and more of the infrared radiation (heat) is trapped inside. (see illustration 2)

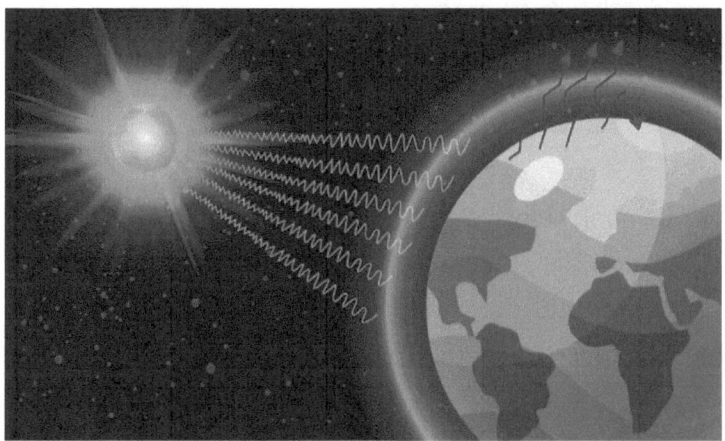

Illustration 1

Imagine having an electric blanket on your bed and then cranking it up to high. Unless it is very cold in your bedroom you may toss the blanket off you after a few minutes or turn down the temperature. But we do not have that option with our atmosphere.

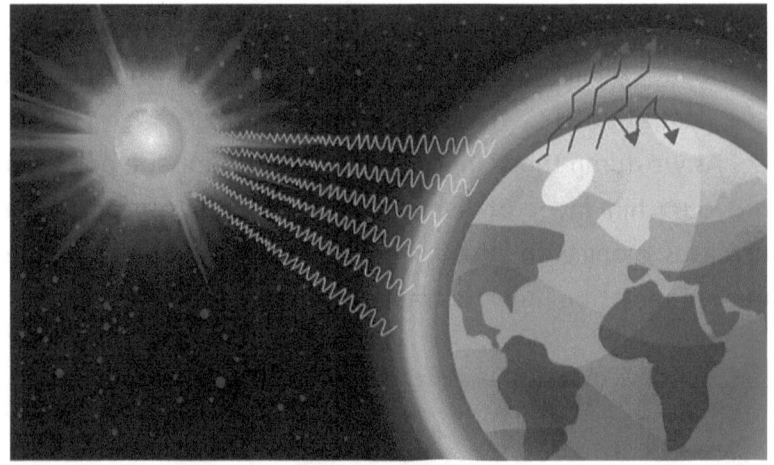

Illustration 2

This book gives you 52 ways to reduce your contribution of CO_2 into the atmosphere. But first we will explore the current effects of the warming planet and what it is doing to our natural systems.

What are Greenhouse Gases?

Think of greenhouse gases as large, very absorbent, sponges. When put into our atmosphere they capture and absorb infrared radiation instead of allowing it to escape back into space. This is causing our atmosphere to heat up, which in turn heats up our air, water, and the earth itself.

There are many sources of greenhouse gas emissions, such as our tail pipes, stacks at the coal powered energy plant, or sources you may never see, like the melting of permafrost in the arctic. In fact, we do not "see" most of it, so it does not seem to be a problem. Imagine if greenhouse gases had a blue or purple tint. Do you think more people would pay closer attention?

This book focuses more on greenhouse gases coming from fossil fuels, which is the largest source of CO_2.

> *Today's atmosphere contains 42% more carbon dioxide than it did at the start of the industrial era. Levels of methane and carbon dioxide are the highest they have been in nearly half a million years.*
> David Suzuki Foundation

There are six main greenhouse gases that are causing global warming. Once they are emitted into our atmosphere they can stay there for decades, centuries, or even millennia, depending on the gas and where it lands.

- **Carbon Dioxide (82%)**
- **Methane (10%)**
- **Nitrous Oxide (6%)**
- Hydrofluorocarbons
- Perfluorocarbons
- Sulphur hexafluoride

The top three are the primary concern because they are closely related to human activities. As you can see, CO_2 is the largest percentage of the mix, and the one we can best reduce by making changes in our daily routines. Let us learn a bit more about the top three.

CO2

Elevated CO2 concentrations in our atmosphere is the biggest problem we are facing today. While we produce our own amounts of CO2 just from breathing, it is the added amounts from the burning of fossil fuels that creates a problem. It appears in just about everything we do in our daily lives, as you can see in the Bonus Video Series.

CO2 has a lifespan of hundreds of years, which means it will be in the atmosphere for many generations to follow. CO2 that entered the atmosphere from your grandfather's car is still up there.

High concentrations of CO2 can displace oxygen in the air. If less oxygen is available to breathe, symptoms such as rapid breathing, rapid heart rate, clumsiness, emotional upsets, and fatigue can result. Since we emit CO2 when we exhale, it is important to be in well ventilated spaces when around large groups of people – such as a classroom or conference center.

Basically, the more CO2 in the atmosphere where we live, the warmer that space becomes. In the Bonus Video Series, you can learn how warming the air, water, and ground affects the very systems we rely on to survive.

Methane

Another greenhouse gas worth mentioning is methane. It has many sources, such as gas escaping from oil and gas wells and landfills. It also comes from decomposition of wetlands, and animal digestion.

Methane, also known as natural gas, is on the top three list because it has a global warming potential that is 21 times greater than CO2, which ranks it among the worst of the greenhouse gases.

While we are not focusing on methane, you should pay attention to the practices of the oil and gas industry and the monitoring of this greenhouse gas entering our atmosphere. We can keep the levels low if we pay attention.

Methane has a lifespan of 12 years. Though this may sound a lot better than CO2, in the first two decades after its release, methane is 84 times more potent than CO2.

Some models show that about 7% of carbon released today will still be in the atmosphere in 100,000 years.

Nitrous Oxide

Nitrous oxide is also emitted during the combustion of fossil fuels and solid waste, from agricultural (fertilizers), and industrial activities like the treatment of wastewater.

While there is a small amount in the atmosphere, it has a lifespan of 114 years and warming potential that is 310 times greater than CO2.

The purpose of this book and Bonus Video Series is to talk about things that affect you and your family's daily lives and offer solutions to empower you to make a change. The focus is

Family Survival Guide

on CO2 levels from the burning of fossil fuels and how it affects the systems within that small space we call home.

I feel it is important for you to understand the interconnectedness of everything on earth and how one little change in your household can affect a mother and her children across the globe.

**Get the Bonus Video Series here:
https://Book.EarthPrintsForFamilies.com

What is a Carbon Footprint?

*car·bon foot·print /ˌkärbən ˈfo͞otprint/
A carbon footprint is historically defined as the total emissions caused by an individual, event, organization, or product, expressed as carbon dioxide equivalent. Wikipedia*

Every purchase we make and every activity we do for our family has a carbon footprint.

The book in your hand (if you are reading a printed copy) was once a tree which was a seed deposited in the dirt as much as 50 - 100 years ago. While it grew it relied on the atmosphere to create the ideal temperatures through all seasons.

The tree relied on the water cycle to provide precipitation at correct amounts. Too little and it would be distressed by drought and be subjected to disease and pests. Too much and it would be threatened by floods and landslides. Conditions were "just right" for it to mature and be harvested.

While the tree is in the ground, it is removing CO2 and other harmful gases, such as sulfur dioxide and carbon monoxide, from the atmosphere, through photosynthesis. During respiration, the plant exhales oxygen.

It inhales the bad and exhales the good. In fact, **one large tree can supply a day's supply of oxygen for four people.**

Carbon is also stored in the soil under those trees. The amount stored is a component of soil organic matter, which is the plant and animal materials that are in the soil in various stages of decay. The world's soils hold approximately twice the amount of carbon than is found above ground in the atmosphere and plants.

Good argument for making sure our soils are kept healthy, right?

Family Survival Guide

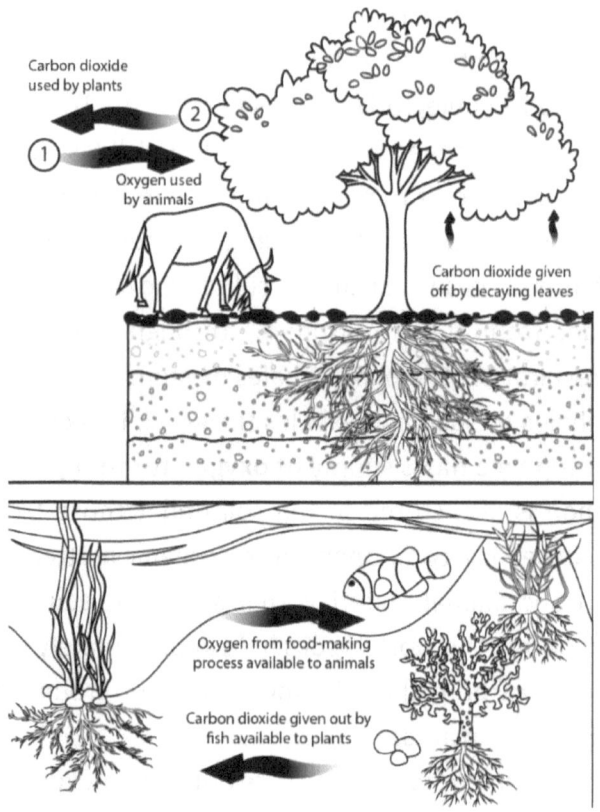

As shown in the illustration, CO2 is used by plants during photosynthesis and the plant releases oxygen that is used by animals and humans.

In water, CO2 is absorbed from the atmosphere and from fish which is then converted into oxygen by aquatic plants. So, the carbon cycle is happening above in the air, and below, in root systems and under water.

Harvesting the tree to make paper for these pages stops this process and releases carbon into the atmosphere. Forest and paper industries replant trees, and sustainable printing practices for books exist to reduce the impacts on our environment.

Fossil fuels are used in every step of the process of making this book. Someone drove to the forest and determined what trees would be harvested. Then someone drove their vehicle to the harvest sites to jump into heavy equipment, powered by diesel, to cut down the trees and put them onto large log trucks which drive to the saw mills or to the coast to be shipped to other regions for processing.

All vehicles are using fossil fuels and emitting CO2 into our thin layer of atmosphere and the air we all need to breathe.

Once the trees are at the processing mill, they are chipped into small pieces. These chips of wood are sent to a paper mill, which can be anywhere in the world, where they are turned into pulp, which also relies on large amounts of water. This pulp can then be turned into paper, which requires large amounts of electricity, to run equipment and heat or cool the facility.

According to the U.S. Energy Information Administration, in 2018, about 63% of our electricity was generated by fossil fuels (coal, natural gas, petroleum, and other gases).

Paper is manufactured into large round bales and shipped to different locations that turn it into different end products - books, newspapers, journals, wrapping paper, cash register

Family Survival Guide

receipts, boxes, and many more. Each application requires more energy for manufacturing and transportation.

At this stage, our book is printed, packaged, and put into cardboard boxes (which has its own carbon journey) and shipped in gas powered vehicles to distribution centers. These are then repackaged in other cardboard boxes and shipped to either a retail store, or to yet another distribution center, where it will be shipped again or drop shipped directly to the consumer.

In our scenario, we are heading to the bookstore to buy this book. Unless we have an electric vehicle that is charged by a renewable source, we are again using fossil fuels and emitting more CO_2 into the atmosphere during our drive there and back.

The total amount of CO_2 this book has put into the atmosphere is difficult to know, but we do know that the pulp and paper sector had direct emissions of about 35.8 metric tons of CO_2 in 2017.

There is much more to the story than just cutting down trees and using recycled paper.

Now, look around you. Every single item in the room you are sitting in has a carbon footprint. It had a long journey through resource exploration, extraction, manufacturing, and transportation, which all use fossil fuels and contribute to greenhouse gasses being emitted into our atmosphere. The longer the journey and different types of components (plastic, paper, metals, etc.), the more CO_2 and other greenhouse gases were created.

Considering the footprint of this simple book, please share it with a friend or library instead of just putting it in the recycle bin (although I hope you keep it as a resource). The carbon journey is long and reducing the need to print more is much better than recycling.

Global Footprints

While China is the largest producer of CO_2, it has been said that approximately one-third of China's emissions are stimulated by the United States demand for exported products.

Data collected in 2015 by the International Energy Agency shows the U.S. has the largest carbon dioxide emissions from fuel combustion at 15.53 metric tons per year per person, and China with 6.59 metric tons, followed by India at 1.58 metric tons. This demonstrates how our personal purchasing decisions affect the rest of the world.

There are many things you can do as a family to reduce your carbon footprint. Each suggestion that follows includes actions to take as a family, and suggested outreach into the community. The more we make this topic part of everyday conversation, the faster we can reduce the impacts of climate change.

Empowering Actions You and Your Family Can Take Now!

These action items were designed to be weekly activities to aid in reducing your family's carbon footprint.

Each of the 52 has a **Take Action Now** section showing suggestions for your family, and for your community. Congratulations for taking this first step!

If you see underlined text, it means there is additional information in the Resource section at the back of the book you can explore.

It will take each of us making simple changes in our daily activities to get to a suggested 50% reduction of emissions by 2030.

You may choose to do one per day, week, or month, but the important thing is to do something. And share with as many people as you can.

Does Your Bank Invest in Fossil Fuel Companies?

It is not something many of us think about, but major banks of the world are supporting the fossil fuel industry to a HUGE degree. If I am trying to reduce my carbon footprint, then maybe it is time to see what my banks are doing with my money. After all, entire countries like Ireland and Norway, are divesting from the fossil fuel companies.

How Do I Know?

Many oil and gas projects go over budget. Who pays for that? In a way I guess some of us do. The world's top banks have put in **$1.9 Trillion** into oil and gas development investments since the IPCC Paris Climate Accord in 2015.

This report by BankTrack shows which banks are the worst offenders. It reports that each year since the Paris Agreement, the amounts of investments keep increasing.

Six of the top 12 worst banks in the world who are investing in fossil fuel development since the Paris Agreement are from the U.S. The top two are U.S. Banks.

Is your bank one of them?

You cannot rely on website information either. Most of those on the list have a page stating how responsible they are - even the top 12 offenders.

Another alarming bit of information is that most 401K accounts invest in the same 9 companies, like Apple, Microsoft, **Exxon Mobile**, and the number one bank offender. What are you invested in?

Solutions

Fortunately, there are resources available to help you make an informed decision about where your money is invested.

The Global Alliance for Banking on Values has a membership of institutions that align with your own personal values.

Another great place to look is the list of B Corporations. Certified B Corporations are a new kind of business "that balances purpose and profit. They are legally required to consider the impact of their decisions on their workers, customers, suppliers, community, and the environment."

Take Action Now!

For Your Family...

Find out if your bank invests in fossil fuels. And if you have a 401K, find out what exactly you are investing in to see if it aligns with your values. If they fail the test, find an institution that does match your values, and be sure to tell everyone about why you changed.

For Your Community...

Share this information with all your family and friends so they too can make informed decision. If you have an environmental responsible investment company in your town, maybe they will give you a presentation.

Together we can make a big statement to our financial institutions that we do not appreciate the use of our money to fund oil and gas developments.

2

Decorating the Landfill

As one holiday passes, decorations for the next one shows up on the shelves. Halloween is replaced with Christmas, which is replaced with Valentine's Day, which is replaced with Easter, and so on. We seem to be in perpetual holiday spending.

According to the National Retail Federation, in 2018 we spent an average of $215 per person on decorations for the winter holidays, followed by $136 per person for Valentine's Day, and $90 per person on Halloween.

Most of those decorations are made from plastic and paper, both of which heavily contribute to our carbon footprint. Should we really cut down trees to make those colorful paper napkins and plates, which are also printed with toxic dyes, that end up in our waterways? They spend the afternoon with you and then end up decorating the landfill.

As you are planning your next celebration you may want to ask yourself some simple questions.

1. What is this item made from? What is the footprint?
2. Will it last for several years and then be donated for reuse?

3. Is it made from renewable resources?
4. Will it just end up in the landfill after the party?
5. Is it biodegradable if put into a compost bin?

Solutions to save you money and the planet

Luckily, there are small changes we can make that have huge impacts to reducing our carbon footprint.

Tableware - Create a "party kit" with reusable plates, utensils, cloth napkins, cloth tablecloths, mugs and cups. You can get a mix of colorful items at a secondhand store and keep them in a tub for each celebration. Don't forget the reusable straws as well.

Goody bags - Just say no to those junky plastic toys that rarely last to the end of the kids' party. One idea might be to have them decorate their own reusable water bottle or t-shirt to take home.

Wrapping Paper - We tend to give presents to the same people each holiday, so starting a cloth bag exchange program may work. Wrap presents in a colorful cloth bag that can be used again by the recipient, and eventually getting back to you. To make a bigger impact, give a set to your family members so they can use them as well. And no taping! Or better yet, give an "experience" instead of stuff.

Balloons - Just say no to balloons. They end up where they should not be. How about reusable, colorful rice paper lanterns?

Family Survival Guide

Cut Flowers - How about a live plant instead? That way it is supplying oxygen and will last a lot longer than cut flowers. You can even include a note that you will help plant in their yard if applicable. And if going outside, make sure it is native to your area.

Lights - when your holiday lights go out, get LED replacements. They last a lot longer and save valuable resources over the years. While the cheap ones are - cheap - they still have a big footprint before they reach the shelf. Plus, there are so many things you can do with the lights, like put them into your empty glass jars and use as table decorations.

Gifts - It is a common theme in this series to give an experience instead of stuff. You can also add edible gifts to that category, heirloom gifts, art, or other consumables.

Take Action Now!

For Your Family...

Start building your Party Kit for all upcoming holidays.

For Your Community...

Suggest to your local associations and/or church that they make some reusable cloth wrapping bags and sell as a fundraiser.

Family Survival Guide

Having an eco-friendly celebration can be easy when you have your reusables at the ready, saving you money and keeping disposables out of the landfill.

3

Compost Reduces Methane

When we send organic waste to the landfill, it is buried and decomposes without oxygen. This results in the production of methane, which is up to 34 times more powerful than carbon dioxide over the following century. With this known fact, why is nearly half of our solid waste produced globally organic or biodegradable?

Landfills do have methane management, at least in developed countries, but it makes more sense to divert organic waste to composting operations. This could be in our own backyards, as community projects, or run by municipalities.

Organic waste needs enough moisture, air, and heat for composting to occur. Burying it daily in a landfill chokes out the air in this process and eliminates the food source for soil microbes (bacteria, protozoa, and fungi) to turn the waste into a valuable fertilizer instead of methane.

Many US Cities have passed Zero Waste goals using the Zero Waste International Alliance as guidance. These include San Francisco, which set the goal for 2020, alongside other large municipalities such as Oakland, Los Angeles, Boulder, Colorado, and Dallas, Texas. Copenhagen, Denmark has not sent organic waste to the landfill in over 25 years.

Composting saves you and your community money by saving landfill space. It creates valuable fertilizer for homeowners and farmers and reduces emissions in the form of methane and added transportation to waste facilities.

According to Project Drawdown,

> In 2015, an estimated 38 percent of food waste was composted in the United States; 57 percent was composted in the European Union. If all lower-income countries reached the U.S. rate and all higher-income countries achieved the E.U. rate, composting could avoid methane emissions from landfills equivalent to 2.3 gigatons of carbon dioxide by 2050.

Take Action Now!

For Your Family...

Call your local municipality or waste management company and ask if they have a composting option. Some may have green waste pickups, but what about household organic waste?

Another thing you can do is plan your meals so that you limit the amount of organic waste you produce during the week. How much do you throw away now?

For Your Community...

Talk with your HOA, city, or county municipalizes about starting a composting facility.

There are many resources available for starting your own compost pile at home. Just do an internet search for "How to Compost" and you will receive tons of ideas.

Carbon Conscious Night Out

While sitting in a local brew pub in Phoenix I looked around and realized a great opportunity to reduce my carbon footprint at this type of establishment. Wait, what?

Let us look first at an abbreviated life cycle of the containers that beer comes in when purchased from the local stores: Aluminum cans and glass bottles, which may or may not be recyclable in your town. (Remember, recycling is not the first filter to look through).

Aluminum

95% of all beer and soft drink cans in the US are made from aluminum. And the amount is staggering, coming in at an average of one can per American per day. Adolf Coors Company manufactured the first aluminum beer can in 1958, which was meant to save money in transportation. Aluminum is much lighter than glass which means more beer on the trucks.

The process is much more complex than what I am adding here, but basically Aluminum is extracted from bauxite ores, which are found in tropical and subtropical regions of the world and imported to the US. This requires the land to be deforested and cleared prior to mining. The minerals go through many processes, which require very high temperatures (as high as 2000° F) and energy consumption along the entire cycle. And let us not forget the waste that is left behind.

According to the U.S. Environmental Protection Agency, many coatings—this includes inks, varnishes and base/rim coats—used by the beverage can industries are heavily concentrated with solvents, which result in large amount of volatile organic compounds (VOC's) being emitted into the air that were harmful and potentially carcinogenic to the human body.

Glass

There are three main raw materials in making a glass beer bottle or pint glass: silica sand, soda ash, and limestone. Of course, energy is used in every step of the mining process. Then the three ingredients are heated to around 2700° F until it turns to liquid.

Imagine how much energy it would take to heat your house to that temp? Water is also used to cool the glass, resulting in wastewater as a byproduct.

Glass is also much heavier than an aluminum can, so shipping of the bottles requires more energy.

I do commend both industries in making great progress in reducing their carbon footprint by light weighting and incorporating recycled materials in the process.

Better Option

Family Survival Guide

So, this brings me back to the local brew pub. In this case, the beer was made right there in the next room. I could see the vats through a glass wall. It's cool to see those shining towers of beer, I guess, since most of the brew pubs I have visited do the same thing.

The beer is then put into reusable kegs (not bottles or aluminum cans) and wheeled (not driven) into the bar area where bartenders pour into reusable glass pints. Patrons also have the option to get a reusable growler to take home and return for subsequent refills.

Can you add up the savings? There is still aluminum (kegs) and glass (pints) used but reused for a long time. Every little bit helps reduce our carbon footprints.

Take Action Now!

For Your Family...

When planning your next party, how about getting some growlers from the local brew pub or a small keg? Then, if needed, head over to your local second-hand store and pick up some glass pints and stick them in your freezer. Or have them bring their own favorite from home. Your guests will love it! Zero Waste.

For Your Community...

Let your local brew pub know that you appreciate the opportunity to enjoy their brews with zero waste and discuss other ways they can reduce their carbon footprint.

It just takes a little extra thought, but the result has great impact on the future, and the present.

Grow It, Don't Mow It

Groomed lawns were first seen at homes of wealthy landowners in 17th century England. Lawns were a sign of wealth and status. Is that why we still have lawns or is it just considered normal? The truth is lawns are a major contributor to our warming climate.

Did you know that lawns are the largest agriculture sector covering 40 million acres in the US? Some of the related issues include the use of home and garden pesticides, fossil fuel requirements, and water.

Pesticides

According to the US EPA, 78 million households in the U.S. use home and garden pesticides. Herbicides are the most used with over 90 million pounds applied on lawns and gardens per year. In fact, suburban lawns and gardens receive more pesticides per acre than agriculture.

This is crazy!

Thirteen of the 30 most common used pesticides at our home are probable or possible carcinogens, 13 are linked to birth defects, 21 with reproductive effects, 15 with neurotoxicity, 26 with liver or kidney damage, 27 are sensitizers and/or irritants, and 11 have potential to disrupt the endocrine (hormonal) system.

On top of that, 17 of the 30 most used are detected in our groundwater.

Fossil Fuel Use in Lawn Care

> *Operating a typical (4 HP) gasoline-powered lawnmower for one hour produces as much smog-forming hydrocarbons as driving an average car between 100 and 200 miles under average conditions. Gasoline-powered string trimmers are more polluting than many lawn mowers.*

One estimate (mindfully.org) states that "the 20,000,000 small engines sold in the U.S. each year contribute about one tenth of the total U.S. mobile source hydrocarbon emissions and are the largest single contributor to these non-road emissions."

Yale University estimates that the US uses more than 600 million gallons of gas to mow and trim lawns per year.

Why do we continue to do something that is so harmful to us and our children?

How about another idea - gardens!

A movement is spreading where people are tearing out lawns and instead putting in flower gardens and organic food.

The cost of organic produce is prohibitive for many families, or not easily available, so growing your own may be an answer.

Gardening has other benefits beyond nutrition, such as bringing families closer together, sharing your bounty with friends, and gives you a sense of empowerment. And just think of how much cleaner your life will be without those pesticides and herbicides.

The idea is to start removing lawn and replace with organically grown food crops and plants to support pollinators, which are threatened by extinction. Seems like a win-win, eh?

This change over may involve some long conversations with your family but the more you discuss it the more it should make sense. If you want to learn more, check out the <u>Food Not Lawns</u> movement for more of the how-to information.

Take Action Now!

For Your Family...

Contact your city to see what their rules might be for creating a garden in your front yard.

For Your Community...

Introduce the idea of growing food instead of lawns with your local groups or write a letter to the editor to share reasons why it makes sense.

Can you imagine a street or area in your neighborhood where several people have converted their lawns to fruit and nut trees and organic produce, and everyone gathers for a harvest party to share the bounty?

6

From the Farm to Your Table

A great new movement is Farm to Table, which means that food is locally sourced and offered by a restaurant (or your own table) directly from the farmer or producer. To make it even better, you may also seek out organic farms.

Somehow, we have strayed away from this way of eating, which was normal not too many years ago, before all the processed food hit the shelves.

Why we should consider Farm to Table

According to a study done by Columbia University, the production of food accounts for 83 percent of greenhouse emissions. It is determined by the amount of fertilizers used that require extensive plowing (by fossil fueled vehicles), or extensive use of irrigation and pesticides. The biggest contributors of greenhouse gas are from non-CO2 types of emissions such as nitrous oxide and methane gas. Both are more potent than CO2.

Meat and dairy accounts for about 150% more greenhouse gas emissions than chicken or fish. A plant-based diet is better for the environment which eliminates the need to grow plants for animal agriculture, but instead grow them for us. Skip the middleman so to speak! The report goes on to say,

"... while buying local food could reduce the average consumer's greenhouse gas emissions by 4-5 percent at best, substituting part of one day a week's worth of calories from red meat and dairy products with chicken, fish, eggs, or vegetables achieves more greenhouse gas reduction than switching to a diet based entirely on locally produced food (which would be impossible anyway)."

Benefits to eating Farm to Table

Farms that follow sustainable practices typically produce lower greenhouse gases, have less nitrogen run-off from fertilizers, and can use less pesticides than the larger farms.

It's also fun to know that the menu will change according to what is available at the time. You may get great, ripe tomatoes in the summer, and fresh winter squash in the fall. The produce would be ripe too since it does not need to be picked early for shipping. It also should be lower priced in many instances, since you are paying the farmer directly, especially in a U-pick situation.

Food Carbon Footprint

There are many benefits to eating locally and organically. Here are just a few.

- US household food consumption emits over 8 metric tons of CO_2 each year, on average. 83% is from the production of food and transportation accounts for about 11%.
- Meat products have a larger carbon footprint per calorie. This is due to the inefficient transformation of plant energy to animal energy. Better to eat from the source!
- You could save the greenhouse gas equivalent of driving 1,000 miles if you were to eat all locally grown food for a year. If you eat a plant-based meal one day a week you could save the equivalent of driving 1,160 miles over the year.
- 30% - 50% less energy is required during production of organic foods but does require more hours of human labor.

Take Action Now!

For Your Family...

Pick one day per week to go all plant-based meals. There are tons of recipes on social sites like Pinterest. I must confess, the vegan options I choose have been much tastier than meat. Or if you eat meat three times a day, try vegetarian meals which often still include eggs and fish.

No need to tell the family what you are making. Just make a tasty meal and they will love it!

For Your Community...

Ask your favorite restaurant to offer more vegetarian and vegan meals that go beyond salads. Remind them it is better for your health, for the environment, and animals.

7

Food on the Go

There is a great movement starting around the globe called Zero Waste Dining. Most of the restaurants are in large cities, but it is time to have that trend filter into the suburbs and smaller towns. Why not?

There are many benefits to becoming zero waste, including reduction in food costs and disposal costs, improving food service practices, and having a positive impact on the environment.

According to an analysis by the Green Restaurant Association, a single restaurant can produce approximately 25,000 to 75,000 pounds of food waste in one year.

How many restaurants are in your town?

While we may not have full control over what your favorite restaurant practices behind the scenes, we do have control of our purchases, especially our to-go box, which is most often made of non-recyclable Styrofoam, a plastic clam shell, or waxed paper board. Do you even eat it the next day or does it end up in the garbage can? Some refer to them as doggy bags, but do you really want to feed your dog people food?

To make things worse, these containers cannot be recycled and must be disposed of in your trash.

When you consider that the average American eats out an average of 4.2 meals per week, these numbers add tremendously to our carbon footprint.

A 2012 study by the Natural Resources Defense Council found that Americans throw away almost half of their food, amounting to $165 billion wasted annually. This is ALL food, not just your own to-go boxes.

Take Action Now!

For Your Family...

Create a to-go kit that includes a reusable container and carry bag. If you are taking it to eat outside of your home or office, be sure to include silverware and napkins. Even better, try to reduce the number of times you eat out.

For Your Community...

Suggest to your local restaurants and buffets to allow reusable containers and to not give you the plastic cutlery, tons of paper napkins, and the plastic bag to carry it all in. Send a letter to your local restaurant association about considering zero waste discussions.

Many states and cities are adopting zero waste practices and request that customers bring their own reusable to-go containers. Just know that due to Food Safety Regulations,

Family Survival Guide

you will need to pack it up yourself. The restaurants responsibility is in the kitchen and their staff, so if you do it yourself, they are protected.

Experiences Instead of Stuff

Seems like every month we have an opportunity to buy a gift for a family member or friend. We scramble to find a last-minute treasure because we ran out of time to make the special personal item that still sits in pieces on the shelf.

Many times, we may just draw a blank on what to get someone who "has everything." You all have that person in your family too. Usually the eldest in the family fall into this category.

Why do we do this? Habit and media ads, I suspect. Especially around the winter holidays, which seem to start before Halloween.

Remember that **every item we buy has a carbon footprint** and is tied to some natural resource. So why would we haphazardly grab something that we think they may like just because we feel we must?

Time to think about getting them experiences instead of stuff. Here are a few ideas to get you started.

- Gift Certificate to a great local restaurant – suggest that you all go together so you can make a nice memory,

instead of them stuffing that new blanket, you though they would like, into the closet.
- Yearly pass to local amusement park – this will go far if the family has young children. It may even bring the kid out of the elders too. You can't buy that at the store.
- Seasonal Pass to your local performing art center, outdoor concert series, or wine tour.

You get the idea. There are unlimited ways to create a memory for your loved ones. In the process you are reducing your carbon footprint and theirs.

Take Action Now!

For Your Family...

Take out your calendar and see what gift buying opportunities are coming up over the next year. If you are organized, you probably have them on the calendar already.

Think of each person. What experience would they enjoy, and will you be able to participate and join in the memory?

For Your Community...

When you get those experiences, share with your community, be it social media or at the next bingo game. Help break those old habits and encourage people to think about the constant bombardment from the media telling us what we need. Wouldn't it be great to have memories instead of stuff?

9

Electric Vehicles Today

Ever driven an electric car? It's a lot of fun. What a thrill it is knowing you can pass up the gas station if you have a full electric model. They will not work for everyone because some people currently have no place to plug them in at home. But charging stations are coming more available each day.

EV's were first re-introduced about ten years ago and now there are over 40 different types from basically every car manufacturer in the world. In 2010 there were only three models available. There were only 1.1 million EV's on U.S. roads as of 2018, but in 2020 there are 10 million worldwide.

Some of the facts about EV's have changed over recent years. Let us clarify and answer some questions you may have:

1. Aren't they more expensive to purchase?

It really depends on the model you choose to buy just like any other car. For example, there are used models with a lower range which are great for city driving and short commutes, especially if you park in a spot that has a free charging station. In 2019, a three year old model with an 85 mile range was available for under $12,000 with 20,000 miles

Family Survival Guide

on the odometer. Of course, you could spend $75,000, or more, if you wanted to. And be sure to check with your state about rebates and federal incentives for new models.

Newer models get 200 - 300 miles on a single charge, which if you have a small commute, just might last you all week. The best part is you no longer need to go to the gas station or get oil changes.

2. What about the battery disposal?

Great news! They are reused and recycled. A big myth is going around about EV batteries being a waste issue, but recent models now use lithium-ion batteries. When they are too worn out to use for driving, they still have 80% charge left that is used by the energy grid to help store power generated by solar and wind turbines. Then at the end of that life they can be <u>dismantled and recycled.</u>

You might want to check out this article about how the scientist who invented the <u>lithium battery just won the Nobel Prize</u> announced on October 9, 2019.

3. Do EV's really cause less air pollution?

Does your state still get most of its electricity from coal powered plants? If so, you might think that plugging into that grid will cause as much pollution as a gas powered vehicle, but in fact, over ten years, an average conventional car will create 66,000 pounds more CO_2 than an electric vehicle charged from the coal-powered grid. If you had solar on your roof and charge your vehicle at home, that number drops even more. That is <u>33 tons more CO2</u> produced by gas powered vehicles over a ten year period! Add in the fact that you no longer need to have oil changes and all the life-cycle pollution that creates from cradle to grave.

4. Can I save money by using an EV?

On average<u> it costs less than half to drive an EV</u> than a conventional fossil burning vehicle. This website has a great tool to determine how much you can save. They have done all the calculations to figure out what the average electricity costs in your state and compared to the average fuel costs. If you have solar on your roof, then you can drop that down quite a bit.

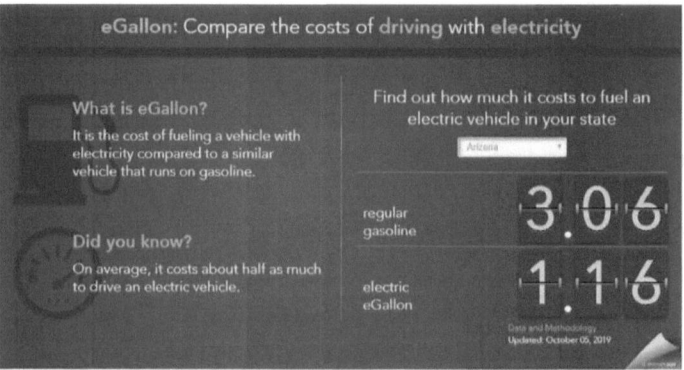

See the difference of pricing for your state.
https://www.energy.gov/eere/electricvehicles/saving-fuel-and-vehicle-costs

Take Action Now!

For Your Family...

Test drive an EV at your local dealers, even if you are not in the market right now. It will send a message that EV's are important to you.

For Your Community...

Use your voice or your pen to ask your local grocery stores, libraries, gyms, work, city parking garages - anywhere you spend time - when they expect to put in Fast EV charging stations.

Let's make EV conversation more common in our local communities. While most people will charge their vehicle overnight at home, we still need to send the message that we want to use EV's and charging stations to keep the air clean for the future of our children.

10

Saga of the Glass Bottle

It is getting harder and harder to recycle glass bottles. Mainly because a lot of the feedstock was headed to foreign markets and they are no longer taking our contaminated materials. Basically, we got lazy. Or maybe recycling education did not reach the customers before they threw all their stuff into the commingle container at the curb.

Let us look at one waste stream – glass.

Glass can be recycled endlessly without loss in quality and purity and glass manufacturers rely on used glass to make new glass. It saves resources.

According to the Glass Packaging Institute, "glass manufacturers require high-quality recycled container glass to meet market demands for new glass containers. Recycled glass is always part of the recipe for glass, and the more that is used, the greater the decrease in energy used in the furnace."

Over a ton of resources is saved for every ton of glass recycled. For every six tons of glass that is recycled we save one ton of CO_2. 80% of all glass containers recovered are re-melted in furnaces and used in the manufacturing of new containers.

Some of the uses for the recycled glass include:

- Bottles and containers
- Construction materials
- Fiberglass
- Astroturf
- Ammunition
- Abrasives
- Matches
- Paint
- Pool filtration mediums

BUT.... Recycling still requires a lot of energy, so it is not the solution.

First thing to consider is opting out of buying glass containers. Remember, recycling is not the best answer. But if we do need to buy glass jars because we love pickles, then finding ways to reuse (after you have reduced) could be an answer. Some ideas for reuse could also eliminate plastic containers, such as making your own salad dressing in one of your used glass jars.

It just takes a little extra thought.

Uses for glass containers are unlimited, but here are a few ideas for the few bottles and jars that do end up in the shopping cart:

- Store dry foods such as beans and rice
- Store refrigerated foods
- Marinate meat

- Make a soap dispenser (put used pump into lid) out of your own soap (also eliminates the plastic soap bottle)
  - Flowers
  - Add an LED light for illuminating the back yard
  - Plant some herbs
  - Leftovers for lunch the next day
  - Load up with cotton balls and essential oils then poke holes in the lid
  - Store those extra buttons that come with new shirts

Also, in the case of pickles, maybe you can purchase the large size jar at a store like Costco. These large jars are especially useful for storing large quantities of things or making iced tea.

Take Action Now!

For Your Family...

Take a survey of what you purchase in glass jars. Is it possible to make it yourself? What could you use those jars for after they are empty?

For Your Community...

If you go to a recycling drop off facility, ask them if there are any local manufacturers using the glass. If you have curbside pickup, call the company, and ask them.

If you want to dig deeper, check out the Glass Packaging Institute. There are also a few bloggers that have ideas for using glass containers in crafts. But it is always better to reduce your usage first.

11

Put Your Mailbox on a Diet

Now that we are more educated about our carbon footprint, do you cringe when you get the mail from the box? How much of it do you just collect because it has always come that way? What percentage gets tossed or recycled? And do we really need file boxes full of invoices from the power company when you can go online to see everything you need?

As I have said before, recycling is not the answer. Switching to electronic statements will prevent the destructive processes that were done to get that advertisement into your mailbox. This includes energy consumption from the point of exploration, extraction of the trees, manufacturing of the paper stock, inks and dies used in printing, and all the transportation at all steps in the process.

I can think of three entities that send a lot of paper: insurance, investments, and banks.

Less and less we see phone books dropped near the front door, or catalogs from some obscure store you must have signed up for and forgot to cancel the print version.

It's just crazy that every year when the phone books come out, a big dumpster shows up at the grocery store so you can recycle them. Why do we accept this?

Most industries today offer a paperless option, mainly because it is much less expensive for them over the long term to create a website versus printing and mailing paper.

According to a study done by <u>Pay It Green</u> back in 2010, if 20% of us switched to electronic statements (and online payment for that matter), we could save over 1.8 million trees. Other savings include:

- Over 150 million pounds of paper
- 2 million tons of greenhouse gasses
- Avoid creating more than a billion gallons of wastewater from the paper mills
- Avoid 100 million gallons of gas required to mail and deliver

In 2007, Dove Consulting completed a study that shows the US Postal Service delivered 19 billion bills which equated to 533 million pounds of paper. It took 235 million gallons of fossil fuels to transport that paper and 1.3 million tons of CO_2.

Take Action Now!

For Your Family...

What is in your mailbox? Switching to paperless statements all at once may be a big chore. But how about one per week? Make a stack and just whittle it away.

If you are still mailing checks, take the time to learn your bank's online system. I know they have one. It is so easy to go in and click a button to make payments.

You may also want to go through your old paper statements and destroy them if the company has all that electronically for you to access. Then use that space for fun stuff.

For Your Community...

If you still receive a phone book, learn how you can stop from receiving it. Share that information with everyone you know!

12

Paper Free Vendors

Wasting paper is worthy of more than one post. This week we are exploring the world of handouts. Those pieces of paper that are handed to you, like flyers and business cards, that you really do not need.

While attending events that are supposedly promoting a greener planet and climate change, vendor tables set up around the perimeter are always full of stacks of papers. These are tables of environmental groups. What is wrong with that picture?

Maybe we take the sheets as a courtesy because we don't want to make them feel that we do not care. But the reality is that they are stuck in an old habit. It is what we have always done.

But we all know that the paper we receive will just end up in the recycling bin or trash most of the time, after it spends a bit of time in the corner on the floor or on the shelf in your office.

The paper production process requires a large amount of energy, with paper and pulp <u>ranked fifth</u> among industries in terms of its energy consumption. This process generates a high level of carbon dioxide emissions, with paper and pulp contributing 9% of all manufacturing CO2 emissions. It also can lead to runoff pollution of water sources, filling of landfills, and deforestation. -Harvard Business School

The good news is that you have the solution in the palm of your hand - the camera on your phone. You can snap a picture of that flyer, event announcement postcard, or business card and retrieve it digitally when you need it. Then just hit the delete button! This also eliminates the need for the obligatory plastic bag that vendors hand out to carry all that paper.

Take Action Now!

For Your Family...

I challenge you to say "No Thank You" to handouts and take a picture instead. Eventually they will get it!

For Your Community...

Talk with any organizations you belong to that have vendor booths. Discuss the option of going paperless. Especially if it is an environmental group! A nice image on the table of what your projects do to help the community is a much better way to use that space and start conversations.

It's time to change the vendor booth paradigm. All we need to know should be on their website. They can create a QR code for you to snap so you can save their website URL or have a large sign with the URL so you can take a picture of it. Plus, they should capture your email address so they can add you to their list and make sure you have a copy of the website address in a day or so, because you just might forget about it.

13

Let There Be Light

Lighting has evolved from the time of Thomas Edison, who invented the first commercially practical incandescent light bulb in 1879. It was revolutionary. Can you imagine how cool it must have been to be able to plug in your first light bulb?

But the incandescent bulb produces light through heating elements that glow, which consumes a lot of energy. Then came the fluorescent lights – the curly ones (Spiral CFL) that caught everyone's attention. They did last longer but did not bring the solutions we need. LED lights are now available and are finally affordable for everyday living.

Which is right for you?

Fluorescent Lights

The first fluorescent light bulb and fixture were displayed to the public at the 1939 New York World's Fair. The spiral CFL was invented in 1976 by Edward E. Hammer, an engineer with General Electric, in response to the 1973 oil crisis. You know the ones - the curly bulbs you still see in old hotel rooms.

But these fluorescent lights take a while to reach full brightness, do not work well in the cold, and contain mercury, which means it becomes a hazardous waste when it is time for disposal. They were said to last 10,000 hours, but after more use it was discovered they only last 6,000 – 8,000 hours, depending on the on/off cycles. This was still better than the 1,000-hour lifespan of the incandescent.

LED

In 1962, GE scientist Nick Holonyak, Jr. created the first practical visible light-emitting diode, known to us today at the LED. These lights have an instant on/off, work well in cold temperatures and have no mercury. Some versions also work well with dimmers. While on/off cycles reduce the life of other lighting options, it does not affect the LED lights, which have an estimated 25,000 hour lifespan. But the best part is that they consume 1/6 the energy over an incandescent bulb.

Not too many years ago these bulbs were a major purchase, but today you can find them for as little as a $1. They save you money as well as greatly reduce your carbon footprint.

Operating Costs

This chart shows the operating costs per type of light bulb. Multiply by the number of light bulbs you have in your home or office and you will see that the savings can be quite substantial when switching to LED lighting.

	Incandescent	LED
Approximate cost per bulb	$1	$1.75
Average lifespan	1,200	25,000
Watts used	60W	8W
# of bulbs needed for 25,000 hours of use	21	1
Total purchase price of bulbs over 23 years	$21	$1.75

CO_2 Emissions comparison

	Incandescent	LED
Power consumption (W)	50	6
KWh (units of electricity used/hour)	0.05	0.006
Hours of operation/day	10	10
Carbon emissions (tons)/year/lamp	0.152083	0.01825
Reduction in carbon footprint (tons/lamp)		0.13383
Lighting carbon emissions (tons)/year/household	6.84375	0.82125
Reduction in carbon footprint (tons)		6.0225

Along with energy consumption savings, switching to LED also brings a reduction of CO_2 emissions into our atmosphere.

Take Action Now!

For Your Family...

Switching to LED lighting is a great way to reduce your energy bill while also reducing your carbon footprint. If you are considering solar for your home or office, your savings could be even greater! We recommend starting with those lights you use the most often, such as in the entryway, kitchen, and main living space.

For Your Community...

Talk to at least one organization you belong to (Church, Service Group, PTO) and ask if they have switched to LED lighting.

With the information presented here, you could give an estimated cost savings over time, and show how much CO_2 is saved in the process. It really is a win-win for everyone. But please be sure the fluorescents are disposed of properly, which does not include putting into city trash receptacles.

Is That New?

How long is your new shirt, new? Until you wash it, right? So why do we always need to buy the newest new thing that is indistinguishable from a used thing after just one washing?

What I am trying to say is that the items you can find in a consignment shop, or secondhand store, are still new to you. Plus, buying things from the consignment shop saves tons of CO2 from entering the atmosphere, and saves you money.

Buying that new shirt from a retail store has a carbon footprint along the entire process – transportation to manufacturing to distribution.

Manufacturing clothes uses a lot of energy, water, dyes, petroleum, and toxic chemical byproducts that threaten the air, land, and waterways. This is especially true in developing countries where most of our clothing is made. Reducing your demand for new clothes will reduce all these threats to our health and environment, cradle to grave.

Donating Clothing

When we are no longer happy with that designer shirt you just had to have last year, consider taking it to a consignment or secondhand store. Reducing your demand for new clothing will reduce your negative contribution to the environment.

One less piece of clothing per person in your household per year will make a huge impact.

When you donate your used clothing and household goods, you are allowing those less fortunate, to buy it. A good example is donating your kids used athletic equipment and clothing. You know how expensive those can be!

Plus, you will eliminate some of the millions of pounds of textile waste that is dumped into our landfills.

Take Action Now!

For Your Family...

When donating clothes, it is better to do so a year or so from the purchase date. Holding on to it just makes it more and more out of style for those who will benefit from buying it at a consignment store.

Look in your closets. What can you donate? AND Say no to at least one item of clothing this year. Do you really need another jacket?

For Your Community...

Work with your local organization or church to host a coat drive, sock drive, glove drive – etc. Or maybe an Eco-Swap where everything is free. There are always people in need in your own community.

15

The Sun May Save You

Solar energy is abundant. In fact, there is enough energy produced by the sun in an hour to provide enough energy for the entire planet for a year. So why are we not using it more?

The commercial and residential building sector accounts for 39% of carbon dioxide (CO_2) emissions in the United States per year, more than any other sector. It is estimated that the average household in the US produces 7.5 tons of CO_2 per year.

Solar is a solution, but it is not for everyone. You do need to own a home. And you need to have the resources to buy it. But most options are zero down with decent credit. Your monthly bill should be close to what you were paying for electricity before you go solar, but you no longer need to pay for your electricity (except a small connection fee). And after a few years, you pay no electric bill! It also adds equity to your home. Win-win.

Now is the best time to get solar on your roof. The investment tax credit (ITC), also known as the federal solar tax credit, allows you to deduct over 20% percent of the cost of installing a solar energy system from your federal taxes. The

ITC applies to both residential and commercial systems, and there is no cap on its value. In 2019 it was 30%, in 2020 it is 26% and goes down each year.

How does it work?

Having the correct number of panels on your roof should eliminate your electric bill, except for a small fee they charge for net metering. Everything inside your home, works just as it did before, but without the CO_2 emissions from your electric source. Panels are getting more and more efficient and last a minimum of 25 years (more like 40).

What is Net Metering?

Electric companies allow you to tie into the grid for a minimal monthly fee. You are in essence using the electric company for your battery. At the present time, having your own battery system to be totally off the grid often doubles the cost of going solar. With net metering, the electric company puts your extra energy generated during daylight hours into the grid and gives you what you need after the sun goes down.

With your own energy plant on the roof you can switch to energy efficient electric appliances and put an electric vehicle in your driveway. This can move you out of the fossil fuel loop all together.

No room on the roof? You may investigate a structure, such as a patio or cover over your parking. Some have been built over chicken coops or other animal shelters. Get creative!

Take Action Now!

For Your Family...

Call up your local solar provider and get a quote- or better yet, get two or three quotes. Not all providers are created equal.

For Your Community...

If you live in a community with an HOA, make sure they know that there is a law that states they cannot prohibit you from choosing solar. Invite a local solar provider to give a presentation to the group. In fact, any group you belong to.

16

The Meat Connection

You may not want to hear this, but eating meat and dairy has tremendous negative impacts to land, water, and our environment. The good news is that reducing or eliminating your consumption of meat can have tremendous positive impacts. With an estimation of 10 billion people on the planet by 2050, scientists are trying to devise a diet plan that will reduce the current impacts of a diet consisting of meat protein.

There are so many statistics and scientific reports on this topic that I thought a list would be an easier way to share.

Impacts of meat and dairy on our planet

Land

- Approximately 43% of the world's ice-free and desert-free land is used to raise livestock. This includes crops to feed them and the cutting down of a lot of trees to house them.
- Plant based diets use 20 times less land to produce than meat production.

- In the US alone, 56 million acres are used to grow feed for animals, while only 4 million acres are growing plants for humans to eat.
- The UN states that it takes up to 10 pounds of grain to produce one pound of meat.

"[A report done by] Science shows that without meat and dairy consumption, global farmland use could be reduced by more than 75% – an area equivalent to the US, China, European Union and Australia combined – and still feed the world. Loss of wild areas to agriculture is the leading cause of the current mass extinction of wildlife."

Water

- A dairy cow requires 50 - 100 gallons of water per day, depending on the weather.
- One gallon of milk requires 683 gallons of water in the entire process.
- One pound of beef requires 2,400 gallons of water. One pound of tofu requires 244 gallons.
- According to the US EPA, animals raised for food in the US produce about 500 million tons of manure a year, which is many times more than the entire human population. But humans have wastewater processing plants. Animals do not. So, it is stored in lagoons that are subject to runoff that pollute our rivers and lakes.

Family Survival Guide

"A vegan diet is probably the single biggest way to reduce your impact on planet Earth, not just greenhouse gases, but global acidification, eutrophication, land use and water use," said Joseph Poore, at the University of Oxford, UK, who led <u>the research</u>. "It is far bigger than cutting down on your flights or buying an electric car," he said, as these only cut greenhouse gas emissions.

Recently we have seen plant based hamburgers and chicken showing up at popular fast food restaurants. Sorry to say, this is not going to change the impact of the beef industry on climate change. It is certainly not healthier either. Hamburgers are made from leftover parts of the cows after they are slaughtered for more expensive cuts. They are also made from dairy cows that have outlived their usefulness. (Their words not mine.) So, the number of cows being slaughtered will not change until we reduce our consumption of meat overall. To make an impact, we need to cut out higher end beef cuts, and wean ourselves off milk and other dairy products.

Take Action Now!

For Your Family...

Stop the consumption of meat at least one day per week. If you want to make tremendous impact, explore veganism, and slowly incorporate that into your daily life.

For Your Community...

Reach out to your favorite restaurants and challenge them to come up with a delicious vegan menu option. Not just salads and beans. There are some fabulous recipes out there that have no meat.

Dropping meat from your menu, or at least reducing consumption dramatically, will not only be healthier for you, but it reduces greenhouse gas emissions and reduces the cruel practices of the meat and dairy industries.

17

The Community Tool Shed

Let's say it is spring. You are getting ready to head down to the hardware store to rent a power washer to do your yearly cleaning, but you stop at the membership warehouse store on the way and see they have one on sale for around $200. Since you pay $50 to rent it, you think you will save money if you have your own.

This is probably true, but the other lens to look through is the cost to the environment. Equipment manufacturing is quite energy intensive. Every product has a carbon footprint. A power washer is basically made of metals and petroleum. Steel box, screws, plastic hoses and containers – you get the picture.

The exact carbon footprint of a typical piece of yard equipment or tool is not easily available, but each step in the process, from exploration of resources, to extraction of minerals and oil, to manufacturing, to distribution, to purchase, uses energy thus adds CO_2 to the atmosphere. Not only from the vehicles that move that stuff around, but also a lot of energy used in the buildings to make the products.

And of course, you need to store it.

A map that shows where all these components come from would circle the globe more than once.

What is an alternative to buying and storing every piece of equipment that you use occasionally?

You may be more comfortable renting or borrowing from a local hardware store as mentioned earlier. Stores offer this service in hopes you will need to buy other parts from them.

But the idea I would love to see become the norm is a Community Tool Shed. You save money, avoid clutter, and shrink your environmental footprint while building community.

The basic concept is that you get together with a few of your neighbors to share things like lawn mowers, snow blowers, extension ladders, tillers, and power washers. A great article on how to do such a project can be seen in this page by EarthEasy.com.

Take Action Now!

For Your Family...

Look around your garage or shed and ask yourself these questions:

What items do I rarely use?

What items do I use daily or weekly?

Are there items you only used once and no longer need?

What can you resell to someone who will use it if you no longer need it?

By reselling or donating your unneeded items, you reduce the number of new items that need to be made, and help others afford items they may not have been able to purchase.

For Your Community...

Invite a few of your favorite friends and neighbors over to discuss the concept of a Community Tool Shed. If you belong to an HOA, how about bringing it up at the next meeting?

18

Sustainable and Conscious Gatherings

Somewhere on your calendar or posted on your fridge is a time for a gathering of some sort. Might be a neighborhood dinner, soccer game, or volunteer group meeting. In most cases there is food involved, right?

I think most of us are on auto pilot when it comes to these gatherings. We pull from our tried and true selections of party food without giving it a second thought as to how it might be affecting our children's future.

Let us focus on just the paper disposables (plates and napkins), which mainly are produced using pulp from virgin wood-based fibers.

As noted by the Sierra Club, "timber production does not harm only trees. A total of 3,000 species of fish and wildlife and 10,000 plant species, including some 300 endangered plant and animal species, live in National Forests in the United States that are open for logging."

If you feel you must use paper products, find the ones made from post-consumer waste, which means it was made from recycled fibers. There are also biodegradable and compost-able sugar cane plates available. Please note that paper plates are not recyclable because they are contaminated with food waste.

Paper plates are not the only thing that needs to be replaced with reusable. Think through all the utensils and dishes that are used. Consider eliminating all throw away items and replacing with reusable.

We had an earlier discussion about the impact of eating meat has on our planet. Your old tried and true recipes may need to be adjusted to include vegetarian or vegan recipes. There are many great options online to choose from. And you do not need to say a word to anyone if it tastes great! Their hearts will thank you too.

Take Action Now!

For Your Family...

Consider visiting a local reuse store and purchasing a variety of small plates, forks, spoons and knives and bowls. You can also get two yards of muslin and cut them into napkin size squares using pinking shears. Put all into a container with a lid so it is easily transported to any event.

Another option is to ask your group to each donate a plate, bowl, silverware, and coffee mug to put into the container. (Maybe they can all chip in a few pennies to buy the container too.) You can also find cloth napkins at the used store.

For Your Community...

Open the discussion about having more sustainable gatherings with all your groups. If there are children involved, get some ideas from them.

Just think of the huge impact this can have on the amount of waste produced and resources used just for your monthly gatherings. It will also save a lot of money over the years. Everyone can share the responsibility of putting the dishes into the dish washer and washing the napkins. Small price to pay for a cleaner future for your children.

19

Say No to Plastic Bags

We used to get the option of "paper or plastic" at the checkout, but now they just start filling up the plastic bags. You grab them and load them into our cars without a second thought. Or do you?

We are seeing more and more images in our news channels about the perils of the plastic bag. Images of turtles laboring to swim because the bags are wrapped around their bodies and eventually drown. Growing pollution from blowing bags that are seen high in the treetops or along fences.

A single plastic bag takes hundreds of years to break down. Bury it in a landfill without sunlight and air and it may take 500 plus years to degrade.

And not just one. Americans use 100 billion plastic bags a year. That is about 1,500 per household. It takes 12 million barrels of oil to make those bags. Think of it this way. For the same amount of gas it takes to create 14 plastic bags you can drive one mile.

Even worse is that 100,000 marine animals are killed by plastic bags annually.

Many states are banning plastic bags, such as California, as well as individual cities. A 2018 UN report shows that at least 127 countries have adopted some form of legislation to regulate plastic bags. So obviously people can adapt to the change.

Take Action Now!

For Your Family...

There are many ways to switch to sustainable alternatives to plastic bags - and not just shopping bags. Take a survey of your day to day use of plastic and see if any of these alternatives might work for you.

- Cloth sandwich bags made from material such as muslin.
- Silicon food bags
- Beeswax cloth wrap
- Reusable Silicon zippered sandwich bags
- Mesh or muslin vegetable bags
- Cloth shopping bags
- Linen bread bags

For Your Community...

Ask your local grocers to consider banning plastic bags or charging for each plastic bag. Most already give a rebate for bringing your own anyway.

20

Your Laundry is Out to Get You

You either love or dread laundry days. Folding can be an art form for some, but others prefer to just leave the clean clothes in the basket. Whatever you choose the impact to the environment can be substantial. The laundry room is one of the largest water-consuming and energy-consuming rooms in any home.

One major impact comes from the electricity it takes to clean your clothes. After the refrigerator, the washer and dryer are big energy hogs and produce approximately 2,400 pounds of CO_2 per year.

Laundry products are also toxic, and those toxins end up in our waterways and in our family's bodies.

A study done by the University of Washington found that "Five of the six products emitted one or more carcinogenic 'hazardous air pollutants,' which are considered by the Environmental Protection Agency to have **no safe** exposure level," according to Anne Steinmann, the study author.

Here is a short list of some of the bad stuff found in laundry detergent:

- Sodium lauryl sulfate

- 1,4-dioxane
- Nonylphenol ethoxylate
- Synthetic fragrances
- Anionic surfactants
- Petroleum distillates
- Phenols
- Optical brighteners
- Sodium hypochlorite bleach
- Ethylene-diamino-tetra-acetate

Not every brand has every item on the list. But they also do not need to list all the ingredients because there is no law that makes them do so. Read that again.

One example is dryer sheets. The Environmental Working Group's senior research and database analyst Samara Geller says that "dryer sheets contain a potentially harmful chemical called quaternary ammonium compounds (QACS)." According to Geller, at the very least it has been known to cause and/or worsen asthma and skin irritations. However, it has also been linked to more serious long-term conditions, like cancer and reproductive issues.

The coating on dryer sheets also make towels less absorbent, which is a towels main job. So why would we use something that reduces their effectiveness?

How do we make laundry day safer for our family?

Detergents:

- Look for products that are "biodegradable" because they usually will not have the top four worst chemicals: 1,4 dioxane, nonylphenol ethoxylate, and sodium lauryl sulfate.
- Look for plant based detergents.

Dryer Sheets:

- Get some wool dryer balls. Not tennis balls or rubber because they leave your clothes smelly.
- Using 4-5 balls per load can cut down your dryer time in half. They create space between your clothes so the air flows better. Plus, it reduces static that occurs from over drying your clothes. This alone could save half a ton of CO_2 per year.

Reduce your energy carbon footprint

In the US it costs approximately 45 cents to dry a load in a 5,600 watt dryer. There are many ways to reduce your energy consumption and save some money at the same time.

Washer

- Choose an energy efficient washer. Most full-sized Energy Star washers use only 8 to 14 gallons of water per load, compared to the 40 gallons used by a standard machine.
- Choose the best size washer for your family

Family Survival Guide

- Use the correct water temperature for washing. About 90 percent of the energy used for washing clothes is spent on heating the water. Most loads can use the cold setting.
- Select an energy-efficient dryer. When it comes time to replace your old dryer, choose an EnergyStar dryer with a moisture sensor which will shut off your machine when clothes are dry.
- Wash only full loads.

Dryer

- Best option is to air dry inside or outside. If you wring the clothes well, they can easily dry on a rack inside. And if you are using a dryer, wringing your clothes out well will cut down your drying time.
- Wash multiple loads in same day. Its more energy efficient to load clothes into a warm dryer.
- Never overload the dryer.
- Keep dryer vents clean.
- If you can skip the iron, do so. It consumes up to 1,800 watts of energy for every two hours it is on and emits nearly 5 pounds of CO_2.

Family Survival Guide

Take Action Now!

For Your Family...

Look through all your laundry detergents and see if they are safe for you and your family. Check the store for plant based varieties or at least biodegradable. They are becoming quite common. Also, hang up a clothesline outside, and/or get a dryer rack for inside.

For Your Community...

If you are in a homeowner's association that does not allow clotheslines, draft a letter, or attend a meeting to explain how environmentally unfriendly and outdated that is. Explain the amount of CO_2 that is emitted by each household/load.

21

What Are Carbon Offsets?

You may have heard that you can buy Carbon Credits or Carbon Offsets, but what does that mean? Both are based on one metric ton of carbon dioxide or greenhouse gases, but there are some differences you may want to know before you start searching for more information.

Carbon Credits are usually issued to companies and organizations that are part of a mandatory national or international carbon market. This may also be referred to as a "Carbon Allowance." On the other hand, Carbon Offsets are voluntary and are preferably purchased after you have already reduced your carbon footprint by other means and are not relying on buying credits to reduce your footprint.

How does it work?

Let's say you are going on a trip and need to fly. Flying is one of the largest emitters of CO_2 into the atmosphere. You may have reduced your carbon footprint at home in many ways, such as getting solar power on your roof, buying an electric car, and making your home energy efficient. But you have no control over the airlines.

Once you know the mileage of your flight, you can go onto a website and purchase Carbon Offsets to cover the emissions produced for the trip. On average, a flight from New York to California is less than $5. That money is used for carbon offset projects such as building wind turbines, solar farms, planting trees, update power plants, and preserving forests.

Find a reputable project

Be aware of the Carbon Offset project you use because there are some bad guys out there. Luckily, there are now regulations that monitor these projects to make sure credits are not used more than once, and that the projects are sustainable.

For example, putting money into a tree planting project does not take into consideration that the trees may burn, be sold for timber, or die before they reach maturity, so supporting a forest preservation project may be better in the long run.

Buying Carbon Offsets does not give license to overindulgence. It is meant to increase awareness of your carbon footprint.

The average American car produces more CO_2 in a year than the total annual production of an average global citizen.

It is clear we need to do more than buy Carbon Offsets.

You may want to dig deeper into this issue to make sure you find a reputable project to work with. Look for certifications by auditors or standards groups like Green-e. Know that there is no fixed price on carbon and the prices will vary per project.

Take Action Now!

For Your Family...

Try this tool to determine your current carbon footprint. Know that this is an estimate as there are many variables. Then, use some of the tips provided in this book to make some changes.

For Your Community...

Bring up the option to meet via an online video conferencing tool such as Zoom for your next meeting. It is not always necessary to have everyone to travel to meet up. If you do meet up, have everyone calculate their mileage and see what impact that single meeting has on your local community.

22

Waste Not so others Want Not

Reports spanning the past 10+ years show that U.S. <u>retail and individual consumers waste 30 - 40%</u> of the average daily calories consumed on a daily basis. That is approximately a pound of food per person, or nearly 150,000 tons of food per day.

Our wasted food still took a lot of resources to produce. In fact, it wastes nearly a quarter of our water supply or over <u>$172 billion in wasted water</u>. The agriculture industry also uses large quantities of fertilizers and herbicides that find their way into our waterways. When the wasted food reaches the landfill, it decomposes and produces methane which is a potent greenhouse gas with 21 times the global warming potential of carbon dioxide.

So why do we have so much waste?

Simple answer is that food is perishable. If not bought from a local farm, it passes through complex supply chains. Along the chain is suffers from damage, contamination, or inefficiencies in harvest, storage, processing, and distribution.

At the home front, we waste food mainly because of poor planning.

Here are some easy ways to reduce your food waste at home which also saves you a little money

1. Shop Smarter - Do not buy more than you need, especially fresh foods. This may require two trips per week instead of one. And plan to use it all up!
2. Store Food Properly - Know how to store your foods so they do not spoil. Some foods should not be stored together while others should not be put into a refrigerator.
3. Eat the uglies too - We tend to root through the bin for the perfect apple. This practice has led to perfectly good food going to waste.
4. Save and eat leftovers - If you store in a clear glass container it is easier to see what is inside.
5. Eat the skin - They are good for you.
6. Make it a smoothie - Great way to use up leftover fruits and veggies, even the wilted herbs and overripe bananas.
7. Add to water - Perk up your water with peels from citrus, apples and cucumbers or wilted herbs. When you are done drinking the water, throw them into the smoothie.
8. Watch serving sizes - Keep portion sizes in a healthy range to limit scraping the leftovers into the garbage can. It is also healthier.
9. Freezer - Some greens that are wilted can be frozen and used in smoothies or soups. Freeze herbs with olive oil

and garlic into ice cube trays to use in soups and sauces. And it is great to have frozen soups or bulk meals on those busy days.
10. Compost if you can.
11. Pack a lunch - It is a great way to use up those leftovers from dinner. Restaurants contribute a lot of food waste.
12. Coffee grounds - They make great fertilizer for plants, are a natural mosquito repellent, and if put into the lawn, will deter female mosquitoes from laying eggs.
13. Pay attention to what you throw away.
14. Donate to food banks and farms - When you have food you know you will not eat before it goes bad, get it to a food bank for those in need.

You get the idea. Think more about how you shop for food, how you store it, and how you can develop a zero waste kitchen.

Take Action Now!

For Your Family...

Once a week sit down and develop a realistic meal plan. Remember the days you will be too busy to cook where those leftovers will come in handy. Then, take that list to the store and do not buy more fresh produce, and meats, than you need.

Family Survival Guide

For Your Community...

Talk to your grocer about offering the "ugly" fruits and veggies. If we do not buy them, they get tossed into the landfill. They are perfectly fine to consume. And your grocer may be able to get a good deal on them and pass on the savings.

Wasting 30 - 40% of our food is unacceptable while over 17 million people in the U.S. go hungry each day.

23

There's oil in my disposable water bottle?

A lot of press has been released about the amount of plastic floating around in our oceans, killing marine life and polluting a valuable resource. One big thing we can do to reduce this problem is to stop buying disposable plastic bottles and replace with a reusable stainless steel bottle.

Those disposable water bottles require enormous amounts of fossil fuels to manufacture and transport around the globe. First, the raw materials to make the bottles are transported in vehicles powered by fossil fuels. The amount of CO_2 and other pollutants depends on how far it has traveled and by what method. This can represent up to 29% of the carbon footprint of the plastic bottle.

Manufacturing of the plastic accounts for the highest percentage of a plastic bottles' footprint. Petroleum hydrocarbon and natural gas are heated to extremely high temperatures in the process. This creates smaller hydrocarbon molecules which are then combined in several different ways. Your water bottle is usually made with a PET resin. The energy needed to produce the PET resin represents about 30% of the carbon footprint of your plastic bottle.

So, we have the resin and now we need more energy to turn that into plastic bottles. It is melted and injected into molds. This accounts for about 8% of the carbon footprint of your water bottle.

Every step takes energy which comes from fossil fuels, including cleaning, filling, storing, and packaging plastic bottles. Waste generation, including carting plastic bottles to landfills, adds to a bottle's carbon footprint. The total of these processes can represent 33% of a plastic bottle's carbon footprint.

- 1 Ton of PET = 3 Tons of CO_2 (30.3 million tons were produced in 2017)
- 1 Liter bottle = 3.4 megajoules of energy
- 1 Liter of water takes 3 Liters to produce

Humans buy 1 Million plastic bottles per minute

Pacific Institute estimates that the total amount of energy embedded in our use of bottled water can be as high as the equivalent of filling a plastic bottle one quarter full of oil.

What about recycling the bottle?

You can see by the above numbers that production of plastic resin is usually the major contributor to the carbon footprint of a plastic bottle. Recycling can reduce carbon dioxide and other greenhouse gasses by an estimated 30 to 70 percent.

Take Action Now!

For Your Family...

The best thing you can do is to purchase a metal reusable bottle and take it everywhere you go!

For Your Community...

When getting drinks, ask for beverages in your own mug and refuse plastic disposable cups. And you might consider getting a reusable straw as well.

We as individuals can make a big difference. Just imagine your favorite coffee shop or lunch spot offering only reusable cups. Think about the numbers presented above. Big impact, right? All you must do is suggest, and maybe some of your friends are doing the same. Plus, the business saves money not buying disposable plastic cups, and on disposing of those items.

Write for your Rights

We Americans have a special weapon that has won battles all over the world – our pen. Among other cherished values, the First Amendment protects freedom of speech and the right for peaceful assembly.

In 2019 we have seen hundreds of thousands of young people taking to the streets sharing their concerns about climate change. It is making a difference in local policy decisions as well as corporations, who are pledging to use 100% renewable energy and other energy reduction practices.

Of all the liberties guaranteed by the First Amendment to the United States Constitution, the most underrated by far is the one that gives us the right to complain to our <u>elected officials</u>. The most effective way to do this is picking up the phone or putting your pen (hands) to paper (keyboard).

There are <u>websites that show contact information for your Representative</u>, State Senators, all the way down to your town mayor.

"Everything is read, every call and voice mail is listened to," Isaiah Akin, the deputy legislative director for Oregon's Senator Ron Wyden, told me. "We don't discriminate when it comes to phone versus e-mail versus letter."

But if you want to make sure you are heard, and influence a lawmaker's opinion, personalized e-mails, personalized letters, and editorials in local newspapers all beat out the telephone. And they are more likely to be read if they are from their constituents.

Take Action Now!

For Your Family...

Go to these websites and identify your Representatives:
- House of Representatives
- U.S Senate

Next, look on your City and County website to find contact information for your local politicians.

Write a letter about an issue you are concerned about (climate change), call and leave a message, send an email, and then send it to your local newspaper as a Letter to the Editor.

For Your Community...

Form or find a group that meets weekly for coffee and write letters. Make sure they are personalized and not just a form letter. Those will be taken more seriously.

25

Gifts of Time

Do the children in your life really need another plastic toy, game, or fad of the month? More than likely, once the wrapping paper hits the trash, the gift is forgotten as they open the next one.

There is no better time than now to put down the electronics and spend quality time together. They will not remember the stuff that was unwrapped over the years, but they will remember those special times spent with family.

Giving the gift of "stuff" has a large footprint. Driving to the store, or ordering online, to find something to give to the child who already has a closet full of faded fads, takes a lot of energy, both human and fossil fuels. The journey from exploration, to resource extraction, to manufacturing, to distribution, produced tons of CO_2 that is now in our atmosphere.

Then there are the trees removed and toxic inks used to produce wrapping paper. And after the item is no longer useful, where does it go? Eventually it is piled up in the landfill and covered with dirt. More energy consumption. All for what?

As parents we want to spend time with our children and build memorable experiences. The first time you do this you may feel a bit strange not having that wrapped box, but the memories will bring so much more joy and provide many health benefits.

According to Dr Margot Sunderland, a child mental health expert, adventurous activities like going on a hike or playing on the beach trigger neurochemicals such as oxytocin and dopamine that "reduce stress and activate warm generous feelings towards each other".

Here are some fun ideas to get you started:

- Present the family with the vacation they always wanted.
- Parent fun days - spending a full day doing fun things with each child per month.
- Grandparents adventure box filled with envelopes containing activities, such as movies, ice skating, shows. Pick one as a surprise!
- Going to local historical locations.
- Pottery classes or other art classes.
- Yearly passes to children's museums.
- Passes to amusement parks near you.
- Weekend getaways to National Parks or nature in general.
- Art, dance, or music lessons
- Putting together a puzzle

You get the idea.

Take Action Now!

For Your Family...

As mentioned in a previous post about giving experiences instead of stuff, create a list of gifts giving dates coming up for the next year. Plan at least one fun experience per month with your family and give it as a gift for the event closest to that date. This will help you take advantage of sales and special pricing days that many venues offer throughout the year.

For Your Community...

Doing this activity with a friend or family member can double your impact. Give suggestions to other family members so the piles of stuff do not continue to grow!

26

Bring Back the Picnic Basket

In previous posts we suggested creating an Event Kit to use for community meetings, and a To Go Kit to use for restaurant left-overs. How fun would it be to bring back the old Picnic Basket to be used for special relaxing moments with your loved one?

It saves you money, reduces waste, and provides an experience to be cherished.

This picnic might just be at a table in a local park, or at a rest stop during a multi-hour trip. Whatever the occasion, it provides time to relax in nature and breathe fresh air.

*Living close to nature and spending time outside has significant and wide-ranging health benefits -- according to new research. A **new report** reveals that exposure to greenspace reduces the risk of type II diabetes, cardiovascular disease, premature death, preterm birth, stress, and high blood pressure.* Science Daily

Your kit can be the pre-packed variety found at home stores, or you can easily create your own in a container you already have. You will need reusable everything - plates, bowls, cups, cutlery, sharp knife, cloth napkins, and extras like corkscrew and wine glasses if you are planning on that romantic picnic. Small salt and pepper shakers are also nice. Just add food and you are ready to go!

Take Action Now!

For Your Family...

Find a suitable container, go through your cupboards to find unbreakable items for the kit, and then head to the secondhand store to fill in the blanks. Once complete, plan a couple of evenings where you and your significant other, or a child, can enjoy a nice relaxing evening in nature.

For Your Community...

Share this idea with friends. Suggest meeting for lunch at a park, a nature trail, or creek side. See how different your conversation can be than those you have had inside a loud restaurant.

27

Driving for Clean Air

If you have a car that uses gasoline or diesel, it is adding to the CO_2 in the atmosphere every time you use it. You know this. But the better you maintain your vehicle, the less fuel you need to use.

In 2018, about 142.86 billion gallons (or about 3.40 billion barrels[1]) of finished motor gasoline were consumed in the United States, an average of about 391.40 million gallons (or 9.32 million barrels) per day. US Energy Information Administration

According to studies done by the US EPA, a typical vehicle emits about 4.6 metric tons of CO_2 per year, based on a vehicle that gets 22 miles per gallon and drives around 11,500 miles per year.

There are many ways to reduce the amount of fuel you use by the way you get around, such as combining trips, using public transportation, carpooling, buying an electric car, etc. But there are other ways you can reduce your fuel consumption. Here are some you may not think about.

Make sure your gas cap is on tight

It is estimated that 147 million gallons of gas is lost to evaporation per year.

Avoid idling

When you are idling at that drive through, you are getting zero miles per gallon. If you idle for more than a minute, turn it off. The EPA estimates that idling for more than 10 seconds uses more fuel that restarting. Better yet, park and go inside!

Clean out your car

The more weight you carry, the lower the fuel efficiency. However, carpooling will always save more fuel than driving individual cars. People are ok but remove all those bags of dog food when you get home from the store.

Improve aerodynamics

When you are not using your roof rack - take it off. Anything you put on your roof will affect the aerodynamics and reduce your fuel economy. Also, driving with the windows closed when going over 35 MPH will give you better mileage.

Clean Dirty Air Filters

This should be part of your oil change. Sometimes the dirt can be knocked off, but every few oil changes you will want to replace them for the best mileage.

Keep Proper Tire Air Pressure

It is amazing how often this can change. Make it a habit to check tires every month, at every oil change, and before big trips. If not properly inflated, you could lose up to 5% of your fuel economy.

Take Action Now!

For Your Family...

Your car should have a recommended maintenance schedule. Pull out your calendar and plug in the important dates. This way you can also save up for them when it is going to be a big expense - like tires and breaks.

For Your Community...

Share this activity with your spouse, siblings, and any grown children who have autos of their own. Talk with local oil change facilities and negotiate a group deal. You could have your own fleet!

Xeriscaping

xe·ri·scape
/ˈzi(ə)rəˌskāp,ˈzerə-/

Xeriscaping is the process of landscaping or gardening that reduces or eliminates the need for supplemental water from irrigation. Wikipedia

In other chapters we talk about replacing your yard with gardens and removing water intensive and chemical dependent lawns. Another option is using xeriscaping which consists of plants that are adapted to droughts and require little maintenance.

Try a little area first before you take out the entire lawn. But have a plan to systematically change to a Xeriscape yard. Why? Because it saves water for people who need it, reduces pollution, saves time and money.

Preserve Water Quality - Less or even no fertilizers and pesticides are needed with Xeriscape. Much of our water pollution comes from urban landscape runoff of these products.

Family Survival Guide

Saves Energy-. A lawn has been shown to reduce home cooling requirements as much as 4 percent compared to a home with no vegetation cover. However, Xeriscape with good tree, shrub and vine placement can cut cooling costs up to 46 percent.

Save Money - Save by reducing the need for water, fertilizer, mowing, seed, and labor. Watering also causes damages to walls and streets. Lawn mowers also damage trees and irrigation systems. You may even see a reduction in your wastewater charges if applicable because you are using less water. Additional savings can come from the lower energy bills when plants are placed strategically around buildings.

Save Landfill Space - A lot of grass clippings are bagged and buried each week.

Save the Air - Lawn mowers, trimmers, blowers, etc. all put pollution into our air. Not to mention the associated noise.

Take Action Now!

For Your Family...

Take a trip to your best plant nursery and ask about Xeriscape plants. Get one at least so you can see how it fits into your landscape. If you like the idea of saving time, money and reducing pollution, talk with the plant nursery about converting a section of your lawn.

For Your Community...

Meet with your HOA, if you have one, or the city, and learn of any restrictions around Xeriscaping. If there are roadblocks, make sure they are aware of the benefits.

Join a Group

There is no need to feel alone in this fight. Thousands of like-minded people around the world are concerned about the climate crisis just as you are. We have families, jobs, and other life commitments.

Meet up with local groups

Each state has a tribe you can join. Many groups meet regularly to share information, have watch parties, participate in rallies, or just talk. If you ever feel a bit overwhelmed, why not reach out? Find a group that resonates with you and try them out. If it is not a good fit, find another one.

Find a group online

Facebook and other social media outlets have special groups you can join. They have discussions, share information, and offer solutions. Just do a search for Environmental Groups in the social media channel search box.

Professional Groups

If you want to have a higher level connection, search for Environmental Groups in LinkedIn. Want to make a difference at work? This is the place to get some ideas and examples of what others are doing.

While you may make changes in your own family, just think of the impact if you are part of a group of individuals that feel the same way you do - a bit overwhelmed by the thought of climate change. Remind yourselves of all the great things that are happening. Share your successes!

Take Action Now!

For Your Family...

Do a simple search to see if there is a group in your area, or online. Attend a meeting - with a friend would be even better!

For Your Community...

Not finding a local group to join? Why not start your own with something as simple as meeting weekly for coffee and discussing things you can do as individuals, as families, and as a community?

30

Give it the Green Business

We have more power than we realize. Our weapon of choice? Our wallets!

We all know that doing business locally is the best way to support your community. But we can make a larger impact and search out those businesses that are "green." What does that mean?

*A sustainable **business**, or a **green business**, is an enterprise that has minimal negative impact, or potentially a positive effect, on the global or local environment, community, society, or economy—a **business** that strives to meet the triple bottom line.* Wikipedia

Businesses that focus on the triple bottom line go beyond just profit. They also consider the social and environmental (or ecological) impacts of their business. So how can you tell if a corporation or business is trying to meet a triple bottom line?

A bit of caution - do not rely on the company's website to tell you how green they are. It is common practice for corporations to do a bit of "greenwashing" which makes them look better than they are. So, you will want to find a specific sustainability report.

If you do not find that on the website, try doing this search in a search engine:

"company name" + "sustainability report" or "company name" + "corporate social responsibility report" or "company name" + "environmental report"

Greenpeace suggest we, "Look beyond advertising claims, read ingredient lists or ask employees about the real skinny on their company's environmental commitment.

Here are three questions you can ask your local business owners/managers:

1. What are you doing to make your business sustainable and/or reduce your carbon footprint?
2. Have you inventoried your carbon emissions and/or energy use?
3. Do you stock/use/make more sustainable or less toxic products?

Take Action Now!

For Your Family...

Pick the five local businesses you visit the most. Maybe it is a chain owned by a local person, or one-of-a-kind shop. Ask them some simple questions about their sustainability policies and be sure to let them know you care about that.

Family Survival Guide

For Your Community...

If you find that your local shops are not informed, talk to your local Chamber of Commerce, or find a chapter of a local Green Chamber of Commerce, and ask for a presentation.

31

Comment Boxes

Many establishments you visit, from Costco to your favorite restaurant, has a comment box. This does not always need to be filled with comments about the food or service.

There are many opportunities in your week to leave a comment.

Restaurants

Do you really need a dozen napkins (trees) and a straw (plastics) with your water? What about those large portions? Restaurants have a large amount of waste and it is often tossed into the trash can without thought. Let us make them aware that we care about this waste.

Grocery

Not everything needs to be wrapped in plastic! They also can highlight the refillable water bottles more than the individual plastic water bottles (which take the equivalent of ⅓ of the bottle size of oil to produce). Some stores even give an incentive for bringing your own bags.

Parking

More and more electric vehicles are on the road, but not enough charging stations. Suggest to places where you spend an hour or so, such as grocery stores, hair/nail salons, and the gym, to put in free EV chargers. Preferably fast chargers. You do not need to have an EV of your own - yet.

Just about every roof can have solar. Every parking lot can have an EV charger. Every store can use LED lighting and programmable thermostats.

Take Action Now!

For Your Family...

Make up a few 3x5 cards that you can leave in the comment boxes. Pick a topic that concerns you the most. Or you can download some I made up for you at our website, https://EnvironmentalGroups.us/resources.

For Your Community...

Share the idea with your family, friends, and community organizations you work with. A group may gather and write up a targeted campaign. Imagine 100 comment cards in your local restaurant asking them to switch to LED lights. Do you think they will listen?

32

Green Hotels

Before you head out for your next trip that requires a hotel stay, consider if they have made any attempts to go "Green."

Hotels use a lot of resources, not only in construction, but in daily operations. For example, on average, a hotel uses 100 to 200 gallons of water per occupied room per day.

What is a Green hotel?

There are basically five practices followed by a hotel that is considered "Green" according to Green City Trips

- They measure and monitor things like energy consumption, water use and waste.
- There is a person or department responsible for sustainability.
- Rooms and services are healthy environments.
- They are eco-smart and innovative. For example, refillable soap dispensers in the showers and water saving fixtures.
- They care about their employees.

Look for Green Hotel Certifications

There are a few certification programs to review for green designation. You will probably find these on their websites, or on plaques in the lobby.

For example, the US EPA Energy Star program reports that on average, hotels in their program use 35% less energy and emit 35% less carbon dioxide than similar buildings.

A Green Seal goes beyond energy. These hotels will have an in-house recycling program, use energy-efficient laundry and kitchen appliances, plus biodegradable cleaning products. And if there is a restaurant, it means they donate leftovers to local food pantries.

LEED (Leadership in Energy and Environmental Design) certification is used for the actual structure. Hotels can earn certified, silver, gold, or platinum LEED status by using recycled building materials, having energy-efficient windows, and meeting a long list of other features. It's possibly the most challenging green hotel certification to achieve.

How to find a Green hotel

An easy way to tell is through Trip-Advisor. They have a Green Leader program under four levels, Bronze, Silver, Gold, or Platinum. You can review the qualifications of each level on the site.

Family Survival Guide

Take Action Now!

For Your Family...

Obviously, if you are planning a vacation over the next year, check to see if the places you will stay are green. This includes hotels, Airbnb, or RV Parks.

For Your Community...

Look up your local Visitor Bureau website and see if they have a section for certified green hotels and restaurants. If not, request that it is added.

33

Eco Swap

If you are like most Americans, you have a bit of "no- longer- needed- stuff" hidden in closets or stacked in the garage. This does not mean it should be destined for the landfill. In fact, your gently used stuff might just help someone in need.

Introducing the Eco-Swap

This is different than your traditional yard sale, which can be quite labor intensive and even agonizing to some. At an Eco-Swap, all items are free. People can bring in their gently used items and swap for others they need.

But there is no requirement to bring anything.

At the end, you take what is left to the local second-hand store where they will sell it.

Location matters

A good place to hold such a swap is near populations that have limited resources versus more affluent neighborhoods. The idea is to offer free household items and clothing to those who could not otherwise afford them - even from the secondhand store.

Your local downtown church or community center would be a great way to find a partner and share their space. They would also have the resources to get the word out to the right people.

All you need are a few tables, a couple of volunteers and your local partners.

Take Action Now!

For Your Family...

Pick a room or closet and start pulling out things you no longer need. One shelf at a time. One drawer at a time. One room at a time.

For Your Community...

Who would be a good partner in your community? Share ideas with them and get it on the calendar. It is that simple. Earth Day is a good time for an Eco-Swap in conjunction with spring cleaning. Maybe fall would be good for holiday decor.

Fast Fashion

Fast fashion is a contemporary term used by fashion retailers for designs that move from catwalk quickly to capture current fashion trends. A second, critical definition adds that fast fashion is not only about quickly moving from runway to store to consumer, but also to the garbage.
<u>Wikipedia</u>

You may have never heard of this term or thought about it while shopping for clothes. But it is a major contributor to pollution and our carbon footprint.

Basically, certain manufacturers and stores take clothes from the runways, and mass produce them very quickly with cheap materials. They are basically thrown away. I think you have all purchased them. They may have a low price, but they do not have a low price when you factor in the effects to our environment - and the unhealthy labor practices it takes to produce them.

Instead of pushing out four seasons, the fast fashion industry has 52 micro seasons. This causes problems all along the process.

*Each year, the clothing that is simply thrown away amounts to about **11 million tons in the US alone**. These garments, full of lead, pesticides, and countless other chemicals, almost never break down and spend their life releasing these toxic chemicals in the air. Fast fashion's carbon footprint is giving huge industries like air travel and oil a "run for their money."* The Good Trade

Fast fashion not only affects our planet, but it also holds hazardous conditions for us humans. Some garments and accessories have shown to have dangerous amounts of lead in them, and exposure to lead increases one's risk of infertility, heart attacks and more.

The cost to humans is also high since it is confirmed that the workers making these garments are underpaid, underfed, and pushed to their limits because there are often few other options.

The human, environmental, and social costs are too high to support the fast fashion industry. So how can we reduce our impact?

- Buy Less - We buy about five times more clothes than our grandparents did.
- Buy from Sustainable Brands - It is a bit more expensive, but if you are buying less it may not be.
- Buy Quality - See what makes a quality product.

- Think twice before throwing out your clothes - repair, donate, recycle instead.
- Buy second hand, swap, rent - more and more opportunities are out there.
- Don't wash as often - <u>Reduce your laundry environmental impact</u>

Take Action Now!

For Your Family...

Best thing you can do is buy less, take care of the items you have, and look for sustainable options. They cost more financially, but with a much lower cost to our environment and the people and communities who make them.

For Your Community...

Ask your local clothing shops where their clothes are made.

35

Battle of the Plants

When planning your next garden, it would be wise to explore the differences between perennial and annual plants.

Perennial plants are those that come back year after year, while annuals need to be replaced each year. Unfortunately, about 80% of our food crops are annuals, yet perennial plants provide a more substantial positive impact on the environment.

Gardeners see advantages to having perennials in their gardens because they are easier to work with and have a life span of several years. Because of this life cycle, they grow much slower than annuals which results in deeper roots which fortify the soil. They also provide ground cover which does not leave the soil exposed part of the year as annual crops do.

Another benefit is that perennials don't need large amounts of nutrients which means less fertilizer, or none, resulting in less toxic runoff. They are also more efficient with their water intake, so rainwater runoff is reduced.

Yet, 80% of our crops are annuals, which are more vulnerable and create insecurity of our overall global food supply.

A small shift to worldwide organic farming may help some of these dilemmas, but presently only accounts for 1% of commercial farmland.

"...a fully developed and mature perennial, poly-cultural farm performs at high nutrient-use efficiencies, regulates the water table, sequester carbon, stabilizes and maintains soil structures, bolsters against extreme weather events, minimizes external inputs such as fertilizers, encourages biodiversity and beneficial insect habitat, and is overall a wise choice in developing a long-term food production culture worldwide." <u>FarmFolio</u>

What are some perennial crops?

You may be wondering what foods to purchase or grow that will promote perennial crops. Here are just a few, which can be a large part of a plant-based diet. Also consider that organic will also have less of an impact on our environment.

- Bananas
- Berries (Raspberries, blueberries, blackberries, etc.)
- Tree Nuts (almonds, walnuts, pecans, cashews, coconuts, etc.)
- Herbs (basil, chives, mint, parsley, sage, rosemary, thyme, etc.)
- Maple

- Fennel
- Leeks
- Artichokes
- Ginger
- Pineapple
- Tree Fruits (Apples, etc.)
- Asparagus
- Rhubarb
- Kale
- Tomato
- Garlic
- Radicchio
- Horseradish
- Globe artichokes
- Avocado
- Dates
- Olives
- Figs
- Grapes

Take Action Now!

For Your Family...

Use the list above to create some favorite meals and snacks and buy organic versions for best impact. If you garden, how many of these can you incorporate into your plan?

For Your Community...

If you are a gardener, learn more about the effects of annuals versus perennials and share with your fellow gardeners. Offer a yearly seed swap of organically grown perennials.

36

Open the Door, Not Just the Window

More and more cities across North America are starting to ban drive through windows for restaurants, banks, groceries, and other locations where the driver does not get out of the car but chooses to idle their engines instead.

These drive-through windows started in St. Louis back in 1930 in the banking industry, where you could drop off your deposits. Now it is common across the world.

As reported by NPR.org, in August of 2019, Minneapolis became the latest city to pass an <u>ordinance</u> banning the construction of new drive-through windows. Similar legislation restricting or banning the ubiquitous windows has also passed in Creve Coeur, Mo.; Long Beach, Calif.; and Fair Haven, N.J.

The reason for the bans? Curbing emissions, reducing litter, improving pedestrian safety, and enhancing walkability.

Carbon Emissions and Idling

A vehicle that uses gasoline or diesel emit gases including carbon dioxide, a major contributor to our changing climate. It also emits harmful pollutants like nitrogen dioxide, carbon monoxide and hydrocarbons.

Auto manufacturers suggest you idle no longer than 30 seconds. <u>US Department of Energy</u> suggests that idling for more than 10 seconds uses more fuel and produces more emissions than restarting your engine. They also report that eliminating the idling of car engines would be equivalent of taking 5 million vehicles off the roads.

Personal-vehicle idling wastes about 3 billion gallons of fuel—
generating around 30 million tons of CO2 annually in the U.S.

US Department of Energy

Pollution kills around 7 million people around the world each year as a result of exposure to air pollution, according to the <u>World Health Organization.</u> That is 13 early deaths every minute.

Take Action Now!

For Your Family...

Park the car and walk inside. Do not forget your reusable mug at the coffee shop!

For Your Community...

Share this with anyone you know that has a car or truck. They will save money and their engine in the process. Win, win for everyone!

37

The Gift of Sight

Millions living in low and middle income countries lack access to basic eye care services. The <u>Lion's Club</u> is a leader in collecting eyeglasses you no longer wear and sending them to people in need. They collect nearly 30 million pairs per year.

You probably have seen collection boxes around town, sponsored by local non-profit organizations or the Lion's themselves.

Of course, they can only send glasses that are still usable, but the good news is that they recycle the frames of those that are not.

They even take those readers you buy at the drugstore.

Though you might be wondering how this all fits into our carbon footprint discussion, please remember the human aspect of the equation. It would be difficult for the recipients to live a productive life without being able to see.

I have said before that recycling is not the final answer, but maybe it is in this case.

Take Action Now!

For Your Family...

If you wear glasses, or know of others who do, locate the places that recycle glasses. Then, gather up all the old pairs laying around in drawers and drop them off.

For Your Community...

You can get your own eyeglass collection box from The Lions Club to use at organizations you belong to. You can also designate an eyeglass collection day and post on social media.

38

Are Your Electronics Hazardous?

Look around you. How many electronics are within sight?

All our electronic gadgets will eventually stop working. Since most are manufactured as a throw-away, instead of repairable, they can become a hazardous addition to our landfills. Electronic waste, also known as e-waste, leach chemicals into the soil that can pollute the groundwater as well as the air.

While e-waste recycling abounds, the majority still end up in landfills.

According to a UN study, over 41.8 million tons of e-waste was discarded worldwide, with only 10%–40% percent of disposals appropriately done.

Fortunately, electronics contain valuable raw materials that can be recycled. Materials include copper, tin, iron, aluminum, titanium, gold, and silver. Electronics also include plastics, glass and other metals that can be recovered, reused, and recycled.

- Apple reported recovering 2,204 pounds (over a ton) of gold worth $40 million from recycling iPhones, Macs, and iPads in 2015.
- According to the EPA, recycling one million laptops saves the energy equivalent of electricity that can run 3,657 U.S. households for a year.
- Recycling one million cell phones can also recover 75 pounds of gold, 772 pounds of silver, 35,274 pounds of copper, and 33 pounds of palladium.

By reclaiming those materials, you remove the need to explore, extract, and process new minerals.

Revisiting the 3 R's

Our used electronics should NEVER go into the trash can, dumpster, or landfill. Consider the entire lifecycle before you make your next purchase.

1. REDUCE the need to replace your electronics as often by purchasing quality products.
2. If you must have the newest tech each year, make sure you can donate the used one so someone can REUSE it.
3. At the end of its useful life, be sure to RECYCLE, or in some cases, trade it in for a new model (such as cell phones).

What can be recycled?

You would be surprised at how much you can recycle.

Best Buy operates the largest retail collection program in the country, having collected and responsibly disposed of more than 1.5 billion pounds of electronics and appliances. And there is no charge to recycle most items.

You can even recycle old cords, cables, VCR's and other technology that has been stacked in your garage since the 70's.

Here is a starting list of items that can be recycled or refurbished. There are probably some things on there you did not know you could recycle.

- TVs,
- Computers, laptops, tablets, servers - all computing devices
- Computer peripherals such as keyboards, cords, wires, cables, and computer mice
- Computer monitors
- Printers and copiers
- Scanners
- Cables
- Circuit boards
- Lamps
- Clocks

- Flashlight
- Calculators
- Phones
- Answering machines
- Digital/video cameras
- Radios and stereos
- Solar panels
- VCRs
- DVD players
- MP3
- CD players
- Motors
- Cell phones can be taken to where you bought it for refurbishing.
- Batteries - Rechargeable only to include: Sealed Lead Acid/computer back-up batteries
- Battery backup systems
- TV satellite equipment
- Computer game assemblies
- Appliances (usually for a fee)

Take Action Now!

For Your Family...

Take inventory of electronics that no longer serve you. If they work, give to a consignment shop, friend, or secondhand store for reuse. If they no longer work, identify the best way to recycle in your community.

For Your Community...

Organize a collection day with a local organization. Partner with a local scrap metal yard and/or e-waste company and you may even use it as a fundraiser, while educating the public on this growing issue.

39

Close, Unplug and Turn Off

There are three simple things you can do at home that will greatly reduce your energy usage, while also reducing the amount of CO2 entering the atmosphere (if you get your electricity from a carbon-based source).

Turn off lights

Maybe you grew up hearing your parents tell you to "turn those lights off." Turning lights off does in fact save electricity, but how much depends on the type of bulbs you use.

You can find out exactly how much energy each bulb consumes by using this calculation:

# of bulbs X watts of bulbs x hours of use per day.
5 bulbs X 60 watts each X 12 hours per day.
300 watts X 12 hours = 3600 watt hours.
To get the kilowatt hours you divide by 1,000. = 3.6 kilowatt hours each day.
3.6 kWh X your cost of electricity (we will average $.10) = $.36 per day or $10.80 per month.

You can plug in your actual watts per bulb and cost per kWh you currently pay to determine the cost and how much you can save by turning them off when not in use.

Incandescent bulbs will use the most electricity while LED's use the least.

Unplug

Appliances that are turned off still pull electricity. Look around you. How many things are plugged in? They do not need the tiny lights to draw power either. Many uses as much power when off as when they are on.

About a quarter of all residential energy consumption is used on devices in idle power mode, according to a study of Northern California by the Natural Resources Defense Council. That means that devices that are "off" or in standby or sleep mode can use up to the equivalent of 50 large power plants' worth of electricity and cost more than $19 billion in electricity bills every year.

It is not just money spent. Production of electricity represents about 37% of CO_2 emissions in the US, which as you know, is a main contributor to climate change.

Some things are not worth it, like unplugging the microwave. Others might benefit by plugging them into a power strip for easy access. But you could start with these 12 things:

- Desktop computers
- Laptop computers
- Televisions
- DVD players and VCRs
- Modems
- Cable TV boxes
- Blenders
- Stereos and radios
- Coffeemakers
- Lamps
- Toasters
- iPods and electronic gadgets sapping energy from a plug-in transformer

According to the U.S. Department of Energy, you could save about 10% on your electricity bill by unplugging unnecessary appliances.

Close the drapes

Having solid drapes or curtains in your home will conserve your energy consumption whether you are in a cold or hot climate.

Glass is a conductor, so heat from inside the house will move to the colder air outside. The colder air that is left next to the glass becomes dense and falls to the floor which draws in new warm air from above. This cycle continues causing your heater to work harder to keep it warm.

According to Energy wise "Good curtains and blinds can reduce heat loss through windows by 60% for single glazed windows, and 40-50% for double glazing."

For those living in warmer environments, curtains also reduce cool air loss. When the sun starts to hit the windows, heat begins to filter in, just as it flows outside in cold weather. Light colored backing on closed curtains will reflect the sun back outside.

According to the U.S. Department of Energy (DOE), white-plastic curtain backing could reduce home heat intake by 33 percent.

Having insulated curtains protects your home for four types of heat loss: conduction, infiltration, convection and radiation. This loss mainly occurs around windows.

So, we play the curtain game. If you leave the house during the day, close the curtains to conserve energy. If you are home, keep them closed when its cold outside, and when it's hot, close them when the sun beats down on them.

An added benefit is that the cost of curtains is a lot lower than purchasing energy efficient windows, which will also reduce heat transfer. But we all don't own the home we live in, so curtains are an easy answer.

Take Action Now!

For Your Family...

Take an inventory of lighting, windows and everything that is plugged in. Plan to reduce your energy consumption in all three areas.

For Your Community...

Brag about how much energy (money) you can save by making these simple changes. Your favorite organizations could also sell LED lights as a fundraiser.

Colorful Hazards

In 2017, 1 ink cartridge per second and 1 million cartridges per day were thrown away. Why does this happen when it is less expensive and easy to have your inkjet cartridges refilled?

As mentioned in many posts, we need to consider the life cycle of every purchase we make. Inkjet ink cartridges are no different. The casings are plastic and steel, which both have large carbon footprints. The ink also has the potential to be harmful to the environment if leached into groundwater.

Some of these ingredients include butyl urea, which prevents your paper from curling; cyclohexanone, which helps ink adhere to polymers; several dyes including reactive red 23 dye, acid yellow 23 dye and direct blue 199 dye, which contains Sulphur; ethoxylated acetylenic diols which modify the surface tension of the water and colors; Ethylenediaminetetraacetic acid (EDTA) which is full of contaminants and ethylene glycol.

But we still put about 375 million of them into landfills each year. And since they take up to 1000 years to decompose (and leach out toxins), you can imagine just how many have been deposited over the past 20 years, and their accumulated affect.

Take Action Now!

For Your Family...

Find locations that refill your type of ink jet cartridges (or other types too). Plus, using less in the first place is always best. Question yourself each time you hit the print button.

For Your Community...

Check with the office staff of your organizations and workplace to see if they are refilling their cartridges. Share how much money they can save by doing so. They will listen.

Experiences for Parents and Grandparents

By the time you are a parent of adults, and become grandparents, you pretty much have everything you need. And if you do not you usually find a way to get it. So, having your family buy you presents can seem a bit frivolous, right? And if you are like me, it is always a chore to figure out what to get because you do not know if they already have it.

Compare these two scenarios.

Scenario One – It is gift giving time for your mom and dad. The ones who raised you, put a roof over your head and kept your belly full. You are crunched for time (because you are now doing the same for your children), so you jump online and start surfing jewelry, wallets, gadgets, etc. You settle on a jewelry box for mom and a wallet for dad for a cost of about $100.

Scenario Two - Instead of surfing the store sites, you start looking at experience sites. You look at museum memberships, tickets to their favorite band, hotels, etc. You decide on a weekend trip to a Bed and Breakfast in a nearby remote location where they can sip coffee by their private, in-room fireplace. Same $100.

Which one do you think they will like better? Which one brings emotion?

The trick is to give a heart-felt gift. Not your heart, but theirs. Something that will create a good memory, not something that will eventually end up in the landfill after it sits in a closet a few years because they do not want to hurt your feelings.

Fine art or homemade gifts also will bring that emotion even though it may technically be stuff. And family pictures are always a hit!

Take Action Now!

For Your Family...

As before, look at the dates on the calendar where you traditionally give gifts to parents and grandparents. Think of their favorite things to do, or something they used to love to do but never find the time to do anymore. Start planning.

For Your Community...

Share this idea with your siblings or other family members and maybe you can pool your money and find a bigger experience for them.

Home Sweet Home

The largest source of greenhouse gas emissions from human activities in the United States is from burning fossil fuels for electricity, heat, and transportation. Looking at the efficiency of our homes can make a big impact on reducing greenhouse gas emissions.

Previous articles discussed the effects of household activities such as handling unwanted mail, food habits, transportation, clothing, lighting, and electronics. A recent study from Environment International found that over 20% of all U.S. emissions are directly attributed to household consumption. If you consider indirect emissions, this figure is closer to 80%.

Energy Audits

A professional energy audit is done by a professional who assesses your home's current energy consumption and supplies you with a report that describes changes you can take to make your home more efficient. By doing so you are reducing your carbon footprint as well as saving money on energy bills.

Professional energy audits can take from 30 minutes to 4 hours, depending on the size of your home.

Here are some common steps to expect of your professional energy auditor:

1. First, they will look around outside to check on windows, walls, and eaves to look for leaks.
2. Then they will look at the attic, if you have one, to inspect insulation and see if there are any unsealed holes.
3. Next stop is your furnace and water heater to determine if they are operating efficiently. They will also inspect ductwork for leaks.
4. Most will do a blower door test, which depressurizes the home to locate leaks, followed using an infrared camera to see where cold air may be leaking.
5. Last stop is lighting. If you are using incandescent bulbs, they will suggest you switch to LEDs, which can save you a lot of money over the years.

Replacing appliances can be costly upfront but the savings will pay for them in just a few years. You can check with your utility and local government to see if they offer low-cost energy efficiency financing or rebates.

Energy Saving Tips

If it is not possible to have a professional energy audit, there are some things you can do yourself to improve energy efficiency in your home.

- Do you have a drafty area? These usually occur around doors, windows, electrical outlets and junctures between walls and ceilings. Seal the leaks using weatherstripping or caulk.
- Inspect the insulation in the attic. Do you have enough?
- Check for leaks around your heating and cooling equipment.
- Switch to LED lighting.
- If it's time for a new refrigerator or other appliance, look for the more energy efficient models.

Your energy bill will show you the savings over the year.

Take Action Now!

For Your Family...

Do a quick energy audit of your home. Make a list of things and complete them as your budget allows. Some are not expensive - lighting and caulk - while others may require a longer wait - insulation.

For Your Community...

Gather four or five family and friends and see if a local professional will give you a break in the cost of audits for all. Buying things in bulk can also save you money.

Put a Blanket on It

Previously articles in this series talked about energy audits of your home, and one of the largest areas you can improve is the insulation which can greatly reduce your carbon footprint.

If you decide to get a professional energy audit, or did a quick audit yourself, you should know the R-value of your insulation. This energy saver tool can help you determine if you have adequate amounts for your location.

Installing insulation in 4 million homes (just 4% of all North American housing stock) is equivalent to the carbon dioxide removed from the atmosphere by planting 667 million acres of trees—10 times the area of Colorado.

Insulation Institute

Where to look for insulation in your home

You may think that the attic is the only place to install insulation, but to be the most efficient, insulation goes from the roof down to the foundation. A list of the six main areas is shown below as presented by energy.gov.

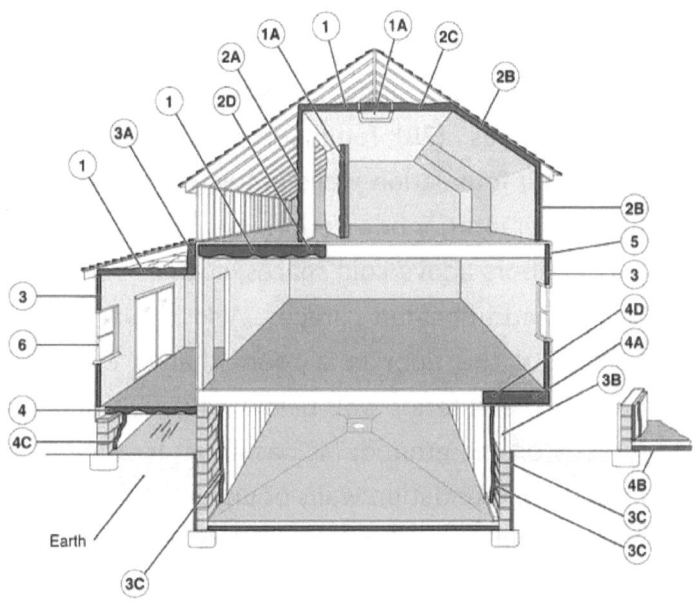

Image credit: Oak Ridge National Laboratory

1. In unfinished attic spaces, insulate between and over the floor joists to seal off living spaces below. If the air distribution is in the attic space, then consider insulating the rafters to move the distribution into the conditioned space.

(1A) Attic access door

2. In finished attic rooms with or without dormer, insulate (2A) between the studs of "knee" walls, (2B) between the studs and rafters of exterior walls and roof, (2C) and ceilings with cold spaces above.

(2D) Extend insulation into joist space to reduce air flows.

3. All exterior walls, including (3A) walls between living spaces and unheated garages, shed roofs, or storage areas; (3B) foundation walls above ground level; (3C) foundation walls in heated basements, full wall either interior or exterior.

4. Floors above cold spaces, such as vented crawl spaces and unheated garages. Also insulate (4A) any portion of the floor in a room that is cantilevered beyond the exterior wall below; (4B) slab floors built directly on the ground; (4C) as an alternative to floor insulation, foundation walls of unvented crawl spaces. (4D) Extend insulation into joist space to reduce air flows.

5. Band joists.

6. Replacement or storm windows and caulk and seal around all windows and doors.

If you have plans to add insulation to your home, please note that there are many types, and not all are environmentally friendly. Remember the entire lifecycle of the products you are considering. Some types that are touted as environmentally friendly include Sheep's Wool, Aerogel, Denim, ThermaCork, Polystyrene, Cellulose, and Icynene.

You can do your own assessment and research to determine what works best in your location.

Take Action Now!

For Your Family...

Get a professional energy audit to find out if you are properly insulated or do research on how to find those answers yourself.

For Your Community...

Talk to your local recycling center and find out if there is a cellulose insulation company in your region and if the local recycled newsprint is used.

Love of your furniture

We have talked about a lot of things in your home, but what about the furniture? If you look around your home, there are various types of wood used in the construction of your furniture, whether it is a solid wood desk, or a leather couch.

When you buy furniture, you have the option to choose the type of wood that is used in the construction. Some are fast growers and somewhat sustainable, while others come from rainforests or old growth forests.

Remember, we look at the entire life cycle of everything we purchase. All wood comes from trees, which produce the air we breathe, sequester carbon, and provides many other benefits to wildlife, humans, and the planet.

Some localized, handmade furniture use more sustainable practices, such as using wood from felled trees in the neighborhood or nearby forests. But commercially produced furniture is not.

So, first, you want to buy quality over price to make the least impact. Then you can ask questions about where the wood came from. Here is a sampling of some popular woods used in making furniture, where they are grown, and the time it takes to grow to maturity.

You can make your own assumptions of the impacts.

- **Sugar Maple** - Vermont and throughout the Northern US and Canada - **12" to 24" per year**
- **Red Oak** - Nova Scotia down through Ontario and into the United States, where it grows from Minnesota down to Oklahoma and east to Arkansas. - **30 years to maturity**
- **Rubberwood - Native to Brazil but comes mainly from Asia** - Rubber plantation trees are generally harvested for wood after they complete the latex producing cycle, when they are 25 to 30 years old.
- Teak - Indonesia - **20-25 years to maturity**
- **Redwood** - Though they once thrived throughout much of the Northern Hemisphere, today redwoods are only found on the coast of central California through southern Oregon - 100 years to maturity
- **Balsam Poplar** - Labrador to Alaska and across the extreme northern U.S. - 10 years
- Bamboo - Northern Australia, India, and Central America - 5 years
- Pine - Northern Hemisphere - 30 - 50 years

These are not exact numbers. For example, some trees grow for hundreds of years before they are harvested.

Life Cycle

As with everything else, it is best to buy quality that will last for many years and can be handed down for years after that. Upholstery can be updated, and solid wood pieces can be refinished. Plan and you can also save money over the years.

Take Action Now!

For Your Family...

Consider refurbishing your old furnishings instead of getting new. Some of us will also find great deals at secondhand stores that can be brought back to life.

For Your Community...

Identify local furniture upholsterers and wood finishers in your community.

Buying for Baby

The beginning of a new life is the perfect time to introduce sustainable living practices.

A traditional baby shower has a room filled with one time use decorations and the usual gifts found in the baby aisle of the local box store: disposable diapers, plastic baby bottles, and three packs of layettes.

But what if we put a little extra thought into the gifts and how they impact not only the health of the baby, but of the planet?

Clothing and other things that touch the skin

Many moms are opting for cloth diapers these days instead of adding to the mounting problems in our landfills.

An estimated 20 billion disposable diapers are added to landfills throughout the country each year, creating about 3.5 million tons of waste. According to a report from the U.S. Environmental Protection Agency, disposable diapers introduce pathogens into the environment from the solid waste they contain.

But let us go beyond the diapers and consider other items of clothing. Consider organic cotton, hemp, or bamboo when purchasing things like these:

- Reusable diapers
- Onesies
- Receiving blankets
- Socks
- Undershirts
- Bibs
- Cloth reusable wipes
- Wool diaper covers

Handmade is cherished

Wrapping a baby in a handmade blanket is a gift that will be cherished for many years. In fact, the blanket will be passed down through the family, or saved by the child and given to their first born.

Items of clothing, such as sweaters and booties, are also found as handmade craft items.

Teething Toys

Most teething toys seem to be made of plastic (petroleum). Why put that in baby's mouth? Another option is wooden rattles and teething rings.

Secondhand Store Finds

Reusing gently used items is a great saving to your wallet as well as the planet. Having your first baby can be expensive when you consider the need for a crib, car seat, stroller, highchairs, and all the other items designed for infants and toddlers.

Buy Quality

If you must buy new, then buy quality. Even if you opt to only have one child, a quality piece of equipment can be sold at secondhand stores, or handed down, and used by others as they begin their journey.

You can also find anything from strollers, car seats, diaper bags, and more, made from recycled materials.

Laundry time

With a new baby you will have more laundry to do. In an earlier article we shared the effects of laundry products on the environment as well as our bodies. Imagine how it affects your babies' tender skin?

There are many plant-based and biodegradable cleaning products on the market today to keep your family safe. Remember that laundry products do not necessarily need to pass FDA regulations. Yet, our skin is our most important organ.

Take Action Now!

For Your Family...

If you know of a baby shower coming up, or you already have small babies in your family, find sustainable, useful gifts.

For Your Community...

Organize an Eco Swap for baby stuff.

Driving Carbon Free

Since transportation is one of the top sectors contributing to CO2 emissions it warrants a little more conversation on the topic.

In the earlier article, we answered some of the myths that form around driving electric vehicles. We found that it costs about half as much to operate, they are affordable, the new batteries are recyclable, and they produce a lot less air pollution.

The article after that was about Carbon Offsets. That is where you give money to a certified organization to offset the pounds or tons of CO2 you produce in your daily life, and they use it to fund projects that reduce CO2 from the atmosphere.

There are many sites out there to purchase carbon offsets, but I found one that funds US projects and a couple of the projects were near me. I got curious about how much CO2 our EV uses versus a gas powered vehicle of similar size.

Here was the result when I plugged the numbers into a carbon offset calculator.

Criteria

The TerraPass website allows you to choose different variables for your carbon offset payment. I wanted to try to get as close as possible when comparing vehicles. Please note that this is not an exact science, but you get the idea.

Both are based on the same zip code, which determines the source of electricity for charging the EV. If you had solar panels on your roof and only charged the EV there, I would imagine that number would be close to zero.

Zip Code: 92401 - San Bernardino, CA
Vehicle Year: 2016
Yearly miles driven: 12,000
EV: Nissan Leaf
Gas Vehicle: Toyota Corolla Automatic

Family Survival Guide

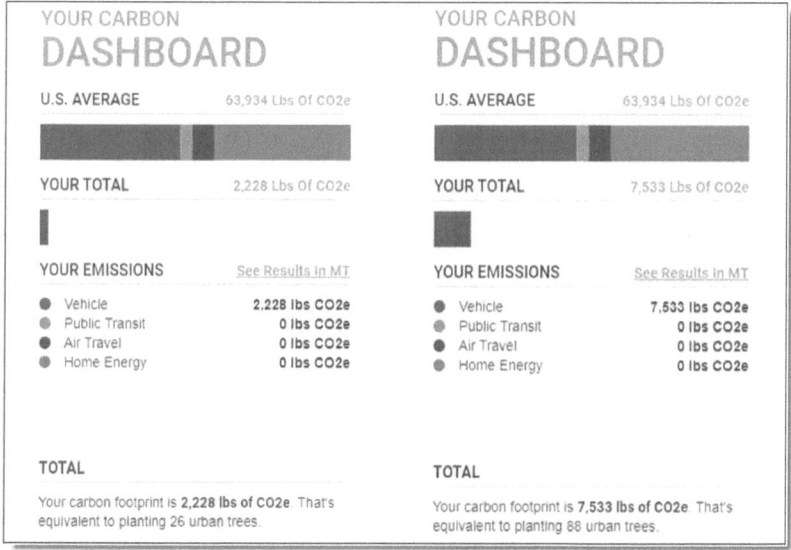

Left is EV, Nissan Leaf.   Right is Toyota Corolla.

Results

You can see that the emissions are about three times as much for the gas powered vehicle versus the EV. You can plug in your zip code and vehicle information to get your numbers.

The calculator on TerraPass also can evaluate other areas of your life where you create CO2.

Please note that I have no affiliation with TerraPass.

Take Action Now!

For Your Family...

If you are looking to purchase a new EV, plug that model into the <u>carbon offset calculator</u> and compare with the car you are currently driving. If you are not yet ready for a new car, go test drive an EV and plug that model into the calculator.

For Your Community...

Share your results on social media so others can also see the impacts of our daily lives and how you can also save money by reducing your carbon emissions.

What is the Deal with Palm Oil?

Palm oil is the world's most edible and affordable oil, but the agricultural practices are not always sustainable. In fact, palm oil production between 1990 and 2008 was responsible for about 8% of the world's deforestation.

It is in just about everything.

It shows up in toothpaste, moisturizer, facewash, shampoos, and conditioners - and that is just in the bathroom. The kitchen cupboards are full of the stuff, from the obvious nut butters, to saltines, energy bars, bread, and even frozen pizza. The more processed, the better chance it contains palm oil.

My ingredients list does not include Palm Oil

Or does it? Here are other ways palm oil are listed in ingredient lists:

INGREDIENTS: Vegetable Oil, Vegetable Fat, Palm Kernel, Palm Kernel Oil, Palm Fruit Oil, Palmate, Palmitate, Palm olein, Glyceryl, Stearate, Stearic Acid, Elaeis Guineensis, Palmitic Acid, Palm Stearine, Palmitoyl Oxostearamide, Palmitoyl Tetrapeptide-3, Sodium Laureth Sulfate, Sodium Lauryl

Sulfate, Sodium Kernelate, Sodium Palm Kernelate, Sodium Lauryl Lactylate/Sulphate, Hydrated Palm Glycerides, Ethyl Palmitate, Octyl Palmitate, Palmityl Alcohol

Look for products with short ingredient lists. For example, bread from a bakery has less ingredients and hopefully no palm oil as compared to packaged breads.

So, what is the big deal?

Palm plantations are mainly in Malaysia and Indonesia, which produces about 90% of the world's supply. In order to grow the palms, the rainforests are burned and cleared. In fact, about 80% of fires in Indonesia are due to palm oil production.

Indonesian tropical forests are treasure troves of biodiversity, holding 10% of the world's species of reptiles, birds, mammals, and fish. Much like the Amazon rainforest, they also store vast amounts of carbon in their soils and trees.

Not to mention the addition of CO_2 put into the atmosphere from the burning, which contributes to climate change.

You can learn more here at Borneo is also burning.

How can we avoid it?

Make sure your products are certified sustainable by organizations such as the Rainforest Alliance or the Roundtable on Sustainable Palm Oil (RSPO).

Eating whole foods is also a safe practice. Plus, it has less of an impact on our environment and is better for your health.

Is all Palm Oil Bad?

Several NGOs, including WWF, the Union of Concerned Scientists, and the Cheyenne Mountain Zoo, issue guides to help consumers make smart decisions about palm oil. However, the certifications don't seem to be working.

Plantations with eco-friendly endorsements have lost 38 per cent of their forest cover since 2007, while non-certified areas have lost 34 per cent, according to researchers from Purdue University in the US state of Indiana.

While it is natural to think that we should avoid palm oil all together, the World Wildlife Fund has this message:
But you don't have to give up products containing palm oil! Avoiding palm oil could have worse effects because it might take support away from companies that are trying hard to improve the situation. This could encourage companies to use other products that may have even more impact on the environment. Palm oil is by far the most efficient vegetable oil to grow as it takes less land to produce than other vegetable oils. **Palm oil can be produced in a responsible manner that respects the environment and the communities where it is commonly grown.**

Take Action Now!

For Your Family...

Read labels and when you can, eat whole foods versus processed foods.

For Your Community...

Educate your groups on the deforestation issues as they relate to palm oil, and suggest you bring only whole foods to group gatherings. This follows the suggestions in precious articles to green up those meetings and make good examples for the members.

Cooling it Down Is Heating Us Up

You may be surprised to know that the number one thing we can eliminate that will make the biggest difference is properly handling refrigerant.

According to the research team that put out the Drawdown project, we can reduce nearly 90 Gigatons of CO_2 in the atmosphere if we switch to a different way of cooling. This includes air conditioning in our homes and transportation, and refrigerators at home, in restaurants, and grocery stores. Anywhere you find appliances cooling things down.

Back in the 80's we found a big hole in our ozone layer - the layer that protects us from UV rays. Thanks to the 1987 Montreal Protocol on Substances That Deplete the Ozone Layer, CFCs (chlorofluorocarbons) and HCFCs (hydrochlorofluorocarbons) were mandated to be completely phased out. This legal mandate was adopted within two years worldwide.

While the suggested replacement, HFCs (hydrofluorocarbons), has minimal effects to the ozone layer, they have a tremendous effect on our warming planet. They warm the atmosphere one thousand to nine thousand times greater than carbon dioxide (CO2). **They are one of the most potent greenhouse gases known to humankind.**

Thankfully, in 2016 more than 170 countries amended the Montreal Protocol to begin the phase out of HFCs as well.

HFC substitutes include natural refrigerants such as propane and ammonia.

When are they hazardous?

Chemical emissions happen throughout the entire life cycle, with 90% of emissions happening at disposal. Luckily, refrigerants can be removed and purified for reuse or transformed into other chemicals that are less harmful.

The older the appliance, the more hazardous it is and can contain other ozone depleting substances.

What is the proper disposal method?

The <u>EPA suggests many programs</u> can be available in your community for proper disposal.

- The store delivering your new appliance may offer a program to collect the old one and properly dispose of it. Make sure where it is going before you do that!
- Municipalities may offer an appliance program at the local landfill, but many require you to have the refrigerant removed first. This should be done by a professional.

- Electric utilities may offer a bounty program where you are paid a "bounty" when a recycler collects and recycles your old appliance. They may also offer rebates and discounts towards a purchase of a new ENERGY STAR® qualified model.

WARNING
Do not attempt to remove refrigerant or compressors yourself. Improperly handled refrigerant may result in physical harm. Only professionally trained individuals using EPA-approved refrigerant recovery equipment should attempt to remove refrigerant from appliances.

Take Action Now!

For Your Family...

Check with your local stores, municipalities, and utility to find out what programs are available in your area. Especially if you are in the market for a new refrigerator or air conditioner.

For Your Community...

When you hear of anyone talking about getting a new air conditioner, appliance or getting their car air conditioner fixed, be sure to share what you have learned here. By acting you will have the answers to share with them.

It May Sound Good at First

Greenwashing has been a part of advertising for many years now. It might show up as a symbol on a box or on the front page of a corporate website. The message is trying to convince you that you are making an environmentally sound purchasing decision. But are you really?

Before digging in, here is a definition of Greenwashing from AZOCleantech that covers the vastness of the practice:

Greenwashing Defined

The misleading act of companies, industries, governments, organizations, and individuals trying to promote unjustified environmentally friendly practices, products, and services through branding, mislabeling, packaging or public relations.

Examples of Greenwashing beyond advertising claims are becoming more and more prevalent and climate change becomes more and more accepted. New programs are springing up in correlation to the recent difficulties with recycling.

One example is a large direct marketing health and wellness company who started a program where you can send back (via mail) your bottles and they will "send" them to a recycler for you, because they have a "special program" with them.

Sorry. Shipping the product to me, then me shipping it back, plus another trip to the recycler is not cutting carbon, but in fact is probably adding to the load.

Another example is a hair care product that comes in a refillable bottle, but you need to mail the empties back to them to refill. Why not send me a refill pouch when I make the initial order, and then send pouches from then on?

Beware of Website Claims

In another chapter we discuss the Greenwashing practices of banking institutions who claim to be a sustainable business on their website, yet they fund the oil and gas industry with trillions of dollars.

Take Action Now!

For Your Family...

When you make a purchase based on a company's claim to be environmentally friendly, do a little more research. Look at products on the grocery shelf a little differently. See how vague the claims are.

For Your Community...

When you find products from the above action, share with your family and friends so they too can understand about greenwashing. Education is the best remedy.

The best thing you can do is think of the entire life cycle of a product, as mentioned several times in this series. That begins at the exploration and manufacturing stage all the way to disposal, be it reuse, recycle, or buried.

50

Be a Trainer

Do you ever feel like you are reinventing the wheel when being environmentally responsible? It is not like we are inventing something new, but in most cases, we are trying to go back in time for a "do-over." Some of the innovations were not the best for us overall.

Instead of looking at it as a battle that you can lose, how about becoming the teacher.

Three Common Classrooms

As mentioned in an earlier article, an easy practice is filling out comment cards for establishments and dropping them on your way out. But taking an active role and becoming the teacher can make a bigger impact on the front lines.

We cannot really fault the workers in these examples because they are in a rhythm of thoughtless habits. But we can snap them out of it!

Grocery Store - If you walk to the checkout with items in your hands, you do not need a bag to take it to the car. Tell the checkout clerk or bagger to please keep the bag. But do not let them put it in the bag first, because then they throw it away. That is something for the comment card box.

It is assumed you bring your own bags when your hands will not handle the purchase. On those occasions when we forget our bags in the car, I just have them put the groceries back in the basket and I bag them outside myself.

Coffee shops - The first thing most coffee shops do after you place the order is pick up a paper cup, which requires a plastic lid and maybe a paper sleeve, so you do not burn your hands.

Since you have your mug with you at all times, hand them the mug to fill for your "to go" order (you are in front of them because you do not use the drive-thru, right?).

You can further educate them by saying "I would rather not produce any waste." And then put your comment in the box about offering real mugs for those "for here" orders.

Restaurants - This is a place that really needs a teacher! Be sure to say, "no straw" and "only one napkin" please. And refuse any refills if you will not be able to drink it all to the bottom before you leave. And have your own mug for any to go drinks.

Again, it is habit for them to keep your glass filled with ice water, but that ice takes a lot of energy to produce.

Take Action Now!

For Your Family...

You no doubt have frustrations with local establishments you visit frequently. Create a few comment cards for each that you can leave one at a time when you visit. And speak out when the opportunity presents itself.

For Your Community...

If you are part of an environmental organization, could your group offer a training course for businesses in your area that address these issues? Does your Chamber offer such trainings?

51

Just Park Already

Entering parking lots is tricky business. It creates the opportunity to waste fuel and put more CO_2 into the atmosphere when searching for the perfect parking spot, driving in circles, or idling in place waiting for someone to pull out.

This may not be your practice, but you know that others do it all day every day in grocery store parking lots around the country.

Other chapters discuss the pollution output for idling and driving, so we will not put those numbers here again.

Why not plan on parking out in the open spaces every time. This allows you to pull in and park without care. Less traffic to deal with and you get a little extra exercise. Less stress. Less fuel used. And less energy used if you drive an electric vehicle.

This assumes you do not need to use the handicap parking, but if you do, you already have a plan to go there first.

Family Survival Guide

Take Action Now!

For Your Family...

Find the entrance to your frequent shopping locations, like the grocery or shopping center, where you will miss all the congestion near the front door. Make a new habit to park out where there are usually spaces available. Easy in, easy out.

For Your Community...

Leave a comment card for those stores to put an EV charging station out in those non congested parking areas, instead of by the front door. You can also share with friends how you park out away from the front door and how much more pleasant it is.

Attention parents!
Your next steps...

Follow us on Facebook -
https://www.facebook.com/EarthFocusGroupUS
Share your experiences, tips, and ideas with other like-minded individuals. Be first to hear announcements of events and challenges.

Do you want to better understand the effects of climate change? You are invited to watch a special Video Presentation titled:

"Preparing Your Family For A Changing Climate"

During this FREE Video Presentation, which is divided into three short modules, you discover the answers every parent needs to know, including:

- → A deeper understanding of climate science 101
- → Effects of Climate Change on natural systems
- → Effects of Climate Change on your family
- → Solutions from around the world that are making a difference
- → What you can do next

So if you're serious about wanting to better understand the effects of climate change and be a super hero to your children, register now for this free video series that shows you why we need to reduce our emissions 50% by 2030.

Get Access Now!

https://Book.EarthPrintsForFamilies.com

Notes

You can find a copy of these citations and other related resources on the Website, where you can click and go!
https://EarthFocusGroup.com/bookresources

What are Greenhouse Gases

https://davidsuzuki.org/what-you-can-do/greenhouse-gases/
https://unfccc.int/kyoto_protocol
https://book2.earthfocusgroup.com/

Global Footprints

https://www.epa.gov/ghgreporting/ghgrp-pulp-and-paper#2017-subsector
https://www.iea.org/
https://www.ucsusa.org/global-warming/science-and-impacts/science/each-countrys-share-of-co2.html1

Does Your Bank Invest in Fossil Fuel Companies?

https://www.banktrack.org/download/banking_on_climate_change_2019_fossil_fuel_finance_report_card/banking_on_climate_change_2019.pdf
http://www.gabv.org/
https://bcorporation.net/

Compost Reduces Methane

http://zwia.org/community-recognition/
http://sfenvironment.org/zero-waste/overview/zero-waste-by-2020

Carbon Conscious Night Out

http://www.designlife-cycle.com/aluminum-soda-cans

Grow It, Don't Mow It

http://www.beyondpesticides.org/lawn/factsheets/30health.pdf
https://mindfully.org
http://www.foodnotlawns.com/

From the Farm to Your Table

https://blogs.ei.columbia.edu/2012/09/04/how-green-is-local-food/

Electric Vehicles today

https://auto.howstuffworks.com/can-electric-car-batteries-be-recycled.htm

https://blog.ucsusa.org/mike-jacobs/lithium-batteries-nobel-prize-win

https://cleantechnica.com/2018/02/19/electric-car-well-to-wheel-emissions-myth/

https://www.energy.gov/eere/electricvehicles/saving-fuel-and-vehicle-costs

Put Your Mailbox on a Diet

http://www.acc.com/legalresources/publications/greenhousecounsel/Encourage-Paperless-Billing.cfm

Paper Free Vendors

http://www.economist.com/news/business/21590965-technological-fix-proposed-combat-global-warming-roll-green-revolution

http://www.greenpressinitiative.org/impacts/climateimpacts.htm

The Meat Connection

https://science.sciencemag.org/content/sci/360/6392/987.full.pdf

The Community Tool Shed

https://learn.eartheasy.com/articles/how-to-start-a-neighborhood-tool-share/

Your Laundry is Out to Get You

https://www.washington.edu/news/2008/07/23/toxic-chemicals-found-in-common-scented-laundry-products-air-fresheners/

What Are Carbon Offsets?

https://www.green-e.org/programs/climate/endorsed-programs
https://www.green-e.org/
https://www.nature.org/en-us/get-involved/how-to-help/consider-your-impact/carbon-calculator

Waste Not so others Want Not

https://www.usda.gov/foodwaste/faqs
https://www.forbes.com/sites/quora/2018/07/18/what-environmental-problems-does-wasting-food-cause/

Write for your Rights

https://www.house.gov/representatives/find-your-representative
http://www.senate.gov/

Bring Back the Picnic Basket

https://www.sciencedaily.com/releases/2018/07/180706102842.htm

Xeriscaping

https://en.wikipedia.org/wiki/Xeriscaping

Join a Group

https://environmentalgroups.us/

Give it the Green Business

https://usgreenchamber.com/

Green Hotels

https://greencitytrips.com/
https://www.energystar.gov/buildings/tools-and-resources/energy-star-score-hotels
https://greenseal.org/
https://new.usgbc.org/leed
https://www.tripadvisor.com/GreenLeaders

Fast Fashion

https://www.thegoodtrade.com/features/what-is-fast-fashion
https://www.huffpost.com/entry/5-truths-the-fast-fashion_b_5690575

https://www.sustainyourstyle.org/en/reducing-our-impact

https://images.squarespace-cdn.com/content/v1/5981c7129f7456741cde6662/1509117624030-BO5DG266R5ZLEQZX6CD2/ke17ZwdGBToddI8pDm48kDaUESuqwRjkxbUsInn7X8cUqsxRUqqbr1mOJYKfIPR7LoDQ9mXPOjoJoqy81S2I8PaoYXhp6HxIwZIk7-Mi3Tsic-L2IOPH3Dwrhl-Ne3Z2Ynh3B3qsoo6BGorFt3NILVGZK_U9dSG2a26HQpn9lcYKMshLAGzx4R3EDFOm1kBS/How+to+recognize+if+a+piece+of+cloth+is+of+good+quality?format=300w

Battle of the Plants

https://permaculturenews.org/2012/06/06/perennial-plants-and-permaculture/

https://farmfolio.net/

Open the Door, Not Just the Window

http://www.minneapolismn.gov/cped/planning/WCMSP-219466

https://afdc.energy.gov/files/u/publication/idling_personal_vehicles.pdf

https://www.who.int/airpollution/en/

The Gift of Sight

https://www.lionsclubs.org/en/resources-for-members/resource-center/recycle-eyeglasses

Are Your Electronics Hazardous?

https://corporate.bestbuy.com/trade-recycle-old-tech-enjoy-new

Close, Unplug and Turn Off

https://www.nrdc.org/sites/default/files/home-idle-load-IP.pdf
https://www.eia.gov/tools/faqs/faq.cfm?id=77&t=3

Home Sweet Home

https://doi.org/10.1016/j.envint.2019.105137

Put a Blanket on It

http://hes.lbl.gov/consumer/
https://insulationinstitute.org/
https://www.energy.gov/energysaver/weatherize/insulation/where-insulate-home

Driving Carbon Free

https://www.terrapass.com/carbon-footprint-calculator

What is the Deal with Palm Oil?

https://www.rainforest-rescue.org/topics/palm-oil/questions-and-answers

https://www.cnn.com/interactive/2019/11/asia/borneo-climate-bomb-intl-hnk/

http://palmoilscorecard.panda.org/

https://www.ucsusa.org/global-warming/stop-deforestation/palm-oil-scorecard-2015%23.XAqmay2ZMdU

http://www.cmzoo.org/index.php/conservation-matters/palm-oil-crisis/

https://www.worldwildlife.org/pages/which-everyday-products-contain-palm-oil

http://d2ouvy59p0dg6k.cloudfront.net/downloads/wwf_position_on_po_boycott_november_2018.pdf

Cooling it Down Is Heating Us Up

https://www.epa.gov/section608/frequently-asked-questions-about-safe-disposal-refrigerated-household-appliances

http://www.energystar.gov/

About the Author

Sandi is the cofounder of Earth Focus Group with a vision of seeing a world of people who understand our changing climate and know that individual actions affect everyone on earth.

She and her husband Wayne travel the US in their motorhome, full time. Staying in places two to three months at a time allows them to explore many natural places and the wonderful people who inhabit them.

Sandi also has a National Park habit and is working towards visiting, exploring, and assisting in the preservation every single one of them.

My Plan to Reduce My Family's Carbon Footprint in the Next 52 Weeks

Family Survival Guide

Family Survival Guide

Made in United States
Troutdale, OR
04/10/2025